People wants the preacher to preach what the people like, but the Lord wants the preacher to preach what the Lord likes. I stick to the word..

Walto's

WALK WITH WORD WORLD WIDE WITHOUT WALLS

Rev. Dr Antony Walto

Book Title: ***Walto's*** **Walk With Word World Wide Without Walls**

Book Author: Rev. Dr Antony Walto

Published By: FOREVER SHININGS

ISBN: 978-93-5605-540-7

About The Author

Rev. Dr Antony Walto is a global Christian ministry leader whose influence spans four continents. Born in Malaysia, holding Indian citizenship, and residing in Dubai, he has dedicated over three decades to religious education and ministry work, accumulating extensive credentials in both business and theological studies. His ministerial journey has taken him across an impressive geographical expanse, covering over 611,821 kilometres by air alone (as of May 2022) and reaching nations throughout Asia, Africa, North America, and Australasia. His work focuses on spiritual leadership development and urban ministry through teaching, preaching, and pastoral care. Dr Walto's academic and professional achievements include multiple doctorates and prestigious recognitions from institutions across the United States and Africa. Notable among these are his Doctor of Divinity degrees from Winchester and Texas, along with his appointment as World Peace Ambassador for both UAE and India. He currently serves as a Director at Grace International Bible University (GIBU) and holds membership on its Board of Trustees. Beyond his professional accomplishments, Dr Walto is a devoted family man. He and his wife, Philomina Walto, are blessed with two children - daughter Leril Manoj and son Shine Morais - along with their spouses Manoj Mathews and Remya Shine. Their family has grown to include three grandchildren: Michelle Manoj, Manshen Manoj, and Stefan Shine. His mission continues to be empowering spiritual leaders and transforming communities through faith-based initiatives and teachings.

About The Book

This book is a profound journey into the depths of faith, exploring the transformative power of the Holy Spirit and God's timeless promises. With compelling narratives drawn from real-life sermons, testimonies, and prophetic messages delivered across continents, it challenges readers to cast aside doubt, embrace faith, and experience divine transformation. Rooted in scripture, the book unfolds the essence of spiritual readiness, obedience, and trust. Each chapter reflects on key biblical teachings, such as the significance of faith, the necessity of surrender, and the unity found in collective prayer and action. Through the lens of personal experiences and global encounters, the author highlights how God's presence manifests in the lives of those willing to cast their nets of faith and prepare their hearts to receive His blessings. This book is not merely a recounting of events but an invitation—a call to action for every believer. It encourages readers to confront their doubts, live out their faith boldly, and participate in God's miraculous works. From spiritual battles to the power of collective worship, the pages resonate with hope, encouragement, and a vision for living a life deeply rooted in God's purpose. Whether you are seeking renewal in your spiritual walk or inspiration to deepen your relationship with God, this book offers practical lessons and profound reflections to ignite your faith and transform your journey with the Lord

Table of Contents

Chapter 1 –

"Take Your Mat and Go Home: Reflections on Mark 2:11"

1. **"Take Your Mat and Go Home" (10 April 2022, USA)**

- **Healing in Action:** The title reflects the central theme of healing, where Jesus commands the paralyzed man to take up his mat and walk home. This symbolizes physical and spiritual restoration.

- **Command of Faith:** The act of picking up the mat is a testament to faith, where Jesus demonstrates His authority over sickness, showing that faith leads to action.

- **Power of Jesus' Word:** The title emphasizes the immediate effect of Jesus' words, where a simple command results in a miraculous healing. His words carry life-changing power.

- **Symbolism of the Mat:** The mat represents a state of helplessness or dependence, and the instruction to "go home" symbolizes a return to wholeness and community after receiving healing.

- **A Personal Journey:** The title suggests an individual and personal experience with Jesus, where the healing is not just physical but also emotional and spiritual, bringing transformation to one's life.

2. Sermon Preached by the Prophet

- **Faith and Healing:** The sermon emphasizes the power of faith in healing. The paralyzed man's faith, along with the faith of those who carried him, resulted in his healing. Faith is portrayed as the key to receiving miracles.

- **The Power of Community:** The four men carrying the paralyzed man represent the strength of community. The Prophet stresses the importance of supporting each other in faith and bringing those in need to Jesus.

- **Taking Responsibility:** The sermon highlights the command to "take your mat," implying that after being healed, there is a responsibility to act, to move forward, and to no longer rely on old habits or dependencies.

- **Spiritual Paralysis:** The Prophet draws a parallel between physical paralysis and spiritual paralysis, encouraging the congregation to rise from their spiritual stagnation and walk in the freedom that Jesus offers.

- **Obedience to God's Word:** The sermon closes with a call for obedience. Just as the man obeyed Jesus' command to rise and walk, believers are urged to listen to God's direction and act on His Word with faith and trust.

3. **Biblical Quote: Mark 2:11 –**
"I tell you, get up, take your mat and go home."

- **Authority of Jesus' Word:** This verse demonstrates Jesus' divine authority. When He speaks, miracles happen. It reminds believers of the transformative power of His words.

- **Call to Action:** The command to "get up" is not just a physical command but a spiritual one, urging believers to rise from their situations and take responsibility for their lives.

- **Faith in Obedience:** The quote shows that healing comes through faith and obedience. The paralyzed man had to believe and act on Jesus' command to experience the miracle.

- **Restoration to Community:** Jesus' instruction to "go home" symbolizes restoration to community and family. It shows that healing brings us back to wholeness and reintegration into society.

- **A Message of Hope:** This verse offers hope to all who feel stuck or paralyzed in life, reminding them that Jesus can change their circumstances with just a word.

4. Prophetic Message

- **Rise from Your Situation:** The prophetic message is a call to rise from situations of despair, sickness, or stagnation. It encourages believers to trust that Jesus can lift them out of their difficulties.

- **Healing in His Name:** The message reinforces that healing—both physical and spiritual—is available to all who call upon the name of Jesus. His power is alive and active.

- **Carrying the Blessing Forward:** Believers are reminded that after receiving healing or a blessing, they are called to carry it forward, symbolized by taking up the mat. It's not enough to be healed; we must also walk in newness of life.

- **Faith that Moves Mountains:** The message highlights the importance of faith, not just for the individual but also for the community. The faith of those around us can be instrumental in our own healing and deliverance.

- **Return to Purpose:** The message ends with a reminder that God's healing brings us back to our purpose. The instruction to "go home" represents a return to living out God's plan for our lives with renewed strength and focus.

5. **Additional Section: "Lessons in Faith and Action"**

- **Faith Beyond Sight:** The healing of the paralyzed man teaches that faith goes beyond what we can see. The men who carried him believed in Jesus' power even before the miracle happened.

- **Overcoming Obstacles:** The sermon shows that faith often requires overcoming obstacles. The men had to find a way to bring the paralyzed man to Jesus, even tearing through the roof to reach Him.

- **Restoration of Dignity:** Taking up the mat and walking is a symbol of restored dignity. Jesus not only healed the man but also restored his ability to live a full life.

- **From Helplessness to Strength:** The paralyzed man's journey represents the transformation from helplessness to strength. Jesus calls us out of our weaknesses and empowers us to walk in victory.

- **Witnessing to Others:** Finally, the healed man became a testimony to those around him. The miracle he experienced was a witness to the power of Jesus, inspiring others to believe and trust in Him.

Chapter 2 -

21 Sept 2016 Sarpeman, Ghana "They need not go, you give them something to eat" (Matthew 14:16)

1. **"You Give Them Something to Eat" - Matthew 14:16 (21 September 2016, Ghana)**

- **Contextual Meaning:** Jesus' instruction highlights the necessity of faith and action in addressing needs, even with limited resources.

- **Dependence on God:** The miracle reminds us of God's power to provide beyond human limitations.

- **Miraculous Multiplication:** It emphasizes surrendering small offerings to God, trusting Him to multiply them for His purpose.

- **Call to Obedience:** Faith and trust in God's instruction lead to miraculous outcomes.

- **Spiritual Perspective:** The miracle points to Jesus as the Bread of Life, offering eternal sustenance.

2. Sermon Preached

- **Faith in Scarcity:** Believers are called to trust God even in lack, knowing He can create abundance.

- **Obedience Leads to Miracles:** The disciples' faith and submission brought about the feeding of thousands.

- **Compassion in Action:** Jesus' love for the crowd inspires us to respond to others' needs with selflessness.

- **Participation in the Miracle:** Our role is to bring what we have and let God work through it.

- **Unity in Purpose:** Working together in faith amplifies the impact of God's mission.

3. Biblical Quote: Matthew 14:16

- **Challenge of Faith:** Jesus' command tests the disciples' trust in His provision.

- **Call to Compassion:** The instruction is born out of love for the people's needs.

- **God's Abundance:** The story reveals that God's resources are limitless when entrusted to Him.

- **Trust in Action:** Faith must be demonstrated through obedience, even when the outcome seems impossible.

- **Eternal Promise:** This act points to the greater spiritual nourishment Jesus provides.

4. **Prophetic Message**

- **Step Out in Faith:** Now is the time to offer what we have, trusting in God's ability to multiply.

- **Focus on What You Have:** God's provision begins with the resources already in your hands.

- **Compassion Leads to Action:** Love must drive our response to others' needs.

- **Promise of Abundance:** Faithful obedience brings not only provision but overflowing blessings.

- **Unity in Mission:** Together, believers can accomplish far greater works for God's Kingdom.

6. **Reflection and Application**

- **Personal Reflection:** Evaluate how you're using your God-given resources.

- **Faith in Action:** Trust God by taking steps of faith, no matter how small.

- **Compassionate Living:** Look for ways to serve others as Christ did.

- **Strength in Unity:** Collaborate with fellow believers to fulfil God's mission.

- **Trust God's Plan:** Believe in His perfect timing and provision for every need.

Chapter 3 –

Signs & Wonders: A Summer Session of Faith and Healing

1. **Sermon by the Prophet:**

- **The Power of Worship:** The sermon began with a vibrant call to worship, encouraging the congregation to praise, sing, and shout Hallelujah as a way to connect with God and invoke His presence.

- **The Role of the Holy Spirit:** The Prophet emphasized the importance of receiving the Holy Spirit, detailing how it leads to the reception of spiritual gifts that strengthen one's faith.

- **Gifts of the Spirit:** He explained the nine spiritual gifts, such as prophecy, wisdom, and speaking in tongues, emphasizing their significance in the lives of believers.

- **The Purpose of Faith:** The Prophet reassured the congregation that faith leads to the fulfilment of divine promises and that believers should remain steadfast in waiting for their spiritual rewards.

- **Spiritual Encouragement:** The message was filled with reassurance, as the Prophet urged people to open their hearts and minds to the Holy Spirit to be blessed with gifts beyond materialistic possessions.

2. Biblical Quote Explanation:

- John 6:67: "Then said Jesus unto the twelve, Will ye also go away?" – The apostle reflected on Jesus' question to His disciples, using it to challenge the congregation on their commitment to faith.

- Acts 2:4: "And they were all filled with the Holy Spirit, and began to speak with other tongues" – This verse was used to explain the event of Pentecost, emphasizing the importance of receiving the Holy Spirit.

- 1 Corinthians 12:5-11: Describing the various spiritual gifts, the apostle highlighted the importance of each gift and how it serves different purposes for believers.

- Matthew 6:1: "Take heed that ye do not your alms before men, to be seen of them" – This was a reminder that acts of faith and charity should come from the heart and not be performed for public approval.

- Mark 10:46-52: The story of the blind man, Bartimaeus, being healed by Jesus was shared to demonstrate the power of persistent faith and how healing can occur through belief.

3. **Prophetic Message:**

- Receiving the Holy Spirit: The apostle prophesied that those who sincerely open themselves to God would receive the Holy Spirit and be blessed with spiritual gifts.
- The Month of Blessings: He declared that the coming month would be filled with spiritual gifts for those who remained faithful and obedient.
- Anointing of Healing: A prophetic word about the gift of healing was given, encouraging individuals to receive the Holy Spirit's power to heal others.
- Breakthrough for Believers: The apostle predicted that believers would experience breakthroughs in their personal lives, including the healing of relationships, financial provision, and spiritual growth.
- Global Influence: He mentioned that those who receive the Holy Spirit would carry their spiritual gifts to the world, proclaiming the Word of God and influencing others globally.

4. Worship Experience:

- A Call to Celebrate: The service was a celebration of faith, filled with music, dancing, and loud praises to God. The congregation was encouraged to worship wholeheartedly.

- Unity in Worship: The apostle stressed the importance of worshipping together as a unified body, with every individual participating through praise, song, and dance.

- Power of Prophetic Worship: Through worship, the apostle suggested that God reveals prophetic messages, healing, and gifts to the congregation.

- The Spirit of Joy: Worship was presented as an act of joy and thanksgiving, with the congregation encouraged to let go of their worries and focus on the blessings of God.

- Spiritual Freedom Through Worship: The message reiterated that true worship brings freedom, not only from personal struggles but also spiritual growth and the reception of divine gifts.

Chapter 4 –

"Cast Your Net: Reflections on Manifestation of the Holy Spirit and Faith" - Jul 26, 2016, South Africa

1. "Be Ready to Receive It" - John 14:26

Contextual Explanation:
The chapter title draws from the verse in John 14:26, where Jesus promises the arrival of the Holy Spirit to guide and teach his followers. This scripture emphasizes readiness, faith, and receptivity to divine intervention. The South African sermon of 2016 builds upon this theme, showcasing a profound spiritual encounter involving the Holy Spirit and addressing the presence of spiritual warfare.

Faith and Obedience:
The narrative begins with the preacher urging the congregation to prepare their hearts to "receive." This symbolizes a spiritual net cast to catch blessings, faith, and grace, reflecting biblical teachings on spiritual readiness.

Manifestation of the Spirit:
The event witnessed physical and spiritual manifestations, demonstrating how faith can confront and overcome the forces of doubt and evil. It highlights the active presence of the Holy Spirit, drawing parallels with biblical moments of divine intervention.

2. Sermon Preached

Personal Testimony:
The preacher shared personal challenges and reflections on their spiritual journey, aligning them with the biblical metaphor of the "net of faith." Stories of perseverance and obedience encouraged listeners to trust in God's provision and timing.

Connection to the Net:
The net symbolizes divine provision and responsibility. As the preacher declared, "The Lord says, I am going to give you a larger net," it signified a call to expand one's faith and readiness to embrace God's blessings.

Spiritual Readiness and Surrender:
Congregants were reminded that the act of surrendering to God, much like casting a net in faith, is crucial for experiencing transformation. The preacher emphasized the importance of relinquishing worldly distractions and embracing spiritual clarity.

3. Biblical Quote: John 14:26, "Be ready to receive it"

Divine Instruction:

The quote reflects Jesus' assurance that the Holy Spirit will equip believers with wisdom, courage, and faith.

Faith in Action:
The sermon illustrated how acts of faith, such as believing in unseen outcomes, allow individuals to overcome challenges and embrace divine intervention.

The Net of Faith:

The net was a recurring metaphor in the sermon, representing faith's capacity to hold God's blessings. The larger the net, the greater the blessings one is prepared to carry.

Manifestation of Divine Power:

The physical and emotional experiences of the congregation—such as tears, spiritual release, and feelings of joy—highlighted the tangible impact of divine encounters.

4. Prophetic Message

Call to Faith:

The preacher declared a prophetic message of hope and renewal, urging believers to trust God's voice. "Will you be able to carry the net?" symbolized the readiness to accept God's will and blessings.

Victory Over Evil:

The sermon emphasized spiritual warfare, calling for believers to rebuke evil forces in Jesus' name. The preacher assured the congregation that the Holy Spirit would shield them, saying, "No evil spirit has to come to you."

Unity in Prayer:

Congregants were encouraged to pray fervently, as collective prayer was seen as a powerful tool to strengthen faith and receive God's blessings.

Encouragement for Growth:
The prophetic words included promises of transformation, deliverance, and divine Favor for those who maintained unwavering faith.

5. Reflection and Application

Personal Reflection:
Congregants were urged to examine their spiritual readiness and moments of doubt. How often do we hesitate to "cast the net" due to fear or uncertainty?

Overcoming Spiritual Battles:
The sermon highlighted the importance of confronting internal and external struggles with faith. Believers were reminded that God's power could overcome any obstacle.

Trusting in God's Plan:
The preacher's repeated declaration, "Be ready to receive it," emphasized patience and trust in divine timing. Believers were encouraged to embrace this message in their daily lives.

Faith as a Lifestyle:
Readers are inspired to adopt a mindset of constant spiritual readiness, cultivating faith, obedience, and surrender in every aspect of life.

Daily Application:
The sermon's teachings encourage practical steps for building faith, such as regular prayer, reading the Word of God, and trusting in the guidance of the Holy Spirit.

Chapter 5 –

6 Oct 2022 Kerala, He was amazed at their lack of faith. Then Jesus went around teaching from the village

1. **"Amazed by Unbelief" (06th October 2022)**

   - **Meaning of the Title:** The title bestows on the theme of Jesus' amazement with people in terms of unbelief at a time when He was performing miracles. Therefore, it gives a premise for really deep reflection on faith and doubt within the lives of believers.

   - **Contrast Between Faith and Unbelief:** This title brings attention to the sharp contrast between the miracles of Jesus and the failure of people to believe, calling for one to reflect on his or her faith.

   - **Importance of Faith in Receiving Miracles:** By emphasizing unbelief, the title serves as a reminder that faith is essential to experience the full operation of God in our lives.

   - **Connection to Personal Reflection:** The title calls the attention of the reader to areas in their life where they see disbelief or doubt instead of believing as they have seen the goodness done by God.

- **Relevance to the Modern Church:** It highlights one common problem that happens to date in churches, namely seeing but not believing, and challenging faith in believers about deepening trust in God.

2. Sermon Preached

- **Jesus' Encounter with Unbelief:** The Reverend begins from the account in Mark 6:6. At this point, Jesus comes to his own place and carries out many miracles; still, he receives unbelief. He concludes by saying that even among the modern believers it has happened the same way.

- **Faith and Action:** He speaks of the relationship between faith and action, "faith without works is dead" and that real faith results in change while non-belief is paralyzing to spiritual growth. He encouraged the congregation to act in faith rather than just to speak about it.

- **Witnessing God's Power:** Being from his own experiences, the preacher would share testimonies about witnessing God's miracles but emphasizes faith as the key to receiving and knowing such miracles in one's life.

- **The Disciples' Role:** He speaks to the disciples, explaining how they are witnesses to the miracles; they heard the teachings, but some of them struggled with a seed of doubt in their lives. He challenges the contemporary Christian to rise above that doubt and become a true disciple by trusting God's word.

- **Call to Overcome Unbelief:** This message calls the church to contend against areas of unbelief. The preacher is urging the congregation to believe that God is more than strong enough to accomplish what He promises, reminding them that inability here limits capacity in the key area to receive His grace freely.

3. **Biblical Quote: Mark 6:6 - "He was amazed at their lack of faith. Then Jesus went around teaching from village to village."**

- **Context of the Verse:** The verse follows the miracles performed by Jesus in His hometown but it did not make the people believe. They knew Him and were aware of His earthly origins so they just could not believe.

- **Link to the Sermon:** The Reverend used this scripture to show how familiarity with Jesus' humanity made Him doubt his divinity with His townspeople; this was a comparison to how contemporary believers might walk blind to God's mighty works in everyday life.

- **Faith as a Gateway:** The verse speaks about the need for faith as a way of receiving God's miracles. Jesus was surprised by the lack of faith, and this is a lesson case to believers.

- **Jesus' Response to Unbelief:** The above quotation shows the way Jesus, though in belief and resistant, continued with His work, teaching and spreading His word to other villages. This can illustrate perseverance in ministry even with opposition and disbelief.

- **Lesson for Believers:** In this, faithlessness was what was challenged before believers to consider the ways in which it might be restraining their experience of God's presence and power, calling them to a more abiding, full trust in Him.

4. **Prophetic Message**

- **Urgency of Faith:** The prophetic message delivered by the preacher is urgent about faith. It is a warning that for one to fully live in God's presence, he or she will need faith.

- **Divine Patience with Unbelief:** While the Lord is patient, the prophecy warns, "Do not test the Lord your God." The word of exhortation in the message is to make their faith in and reliance upon the Lord strong.

- **Call to Spiritual Revival:** The Reverend is calling for a religious revival that's inviting believers to return their spirits to the Holy Spirit. This is prophecy, where God pours His spirit but only over those who believe.

- **Healing and Miracles:** The prophecy promises healing and miracles that will follow those who perfectly believe. The preacher asserts that, just as Jesus healed back in his time, miracles are also available to people who have faith today.

- **Divine Instruction:** The prophetic word concludes by calling up believers to follow the divinity's instruction without hesitation. The church is encouraged to walk in faith and assured that in this way, God will lead them through all challenges.

5. **Lessons for Believers**

- **Understanding the Role of Doubt:** This section encourages the readers to reflect and face their doubts. Thereby, they can understand that disbelief can block their relationship with God. It invites them to ponder on the cause of unbelief and to call for resolution through prayer and study of the Word.

- **Faith as a Daily Practice:** Faith is again, therefore, not an act done at one time but a daily exercise for believers. The chapter continues to espouse that continued trust in God is important in any phase of life.

- **Recognizing God's Power:** The chapter provokes readers to open their eyes to the miracles happening in their lives and see that God's hand is powerful behind the daily events of life. It challenges them to cultivate gratitude in the hearts of men while God continues working.

- **Responding to God's Word:** The believers are notified that faith without works is dead. This section challenges the believers to work according to faith through obedience to God's instructions and living according to His will.

- **Encouragement for Spiritual Growth:** This final section of the book thus gives practical advice in terms of how to attain spiritual growth. It encourages believers to pray regularly, attend fellowship meetings, and study the Bible. This book assures believers that as they grow in faith, there will be a realization of even more miracles of God happening in their lives.

Chapter 6- Liverpool Bethel Church, Australia. 27th April 2014

1. The Sermon Preached by the Apostle

a) **Introduction to Divine Calling:**
The apostle begins by emphasizing the importance of recognizing and responding to God's call. He mentions that many believers are chosen for a specific purpose but are hesitant to act upon it. The call is not just an invitation but a command to fulfil God's work.

b) **The Concept of Leaving the World Behind:**
The message of not loving the world or worldly possessions is highlighted. The apostle preaches that loving the material world distances believers from God's grace. Only by detaching from earthly desires can one truly follow the path God has set.

c) **The Role of Faith in Difficult Times:**
Faith is presented as the cornerstone of the believer's relationship with God. The apostle shares personal anecdotes and experiences, demonstrating how faith has led to miraculous interventions, even in the most challenging circumstances.

d) **Obedience as a Sign of True Faith:**
Obedience to God's word, even when it seems difficult or irrational, is described as the true test of faith. The apostle recounts instances from scripture and his own life where obeying God's commands led to spiritual and physical deliverance.

e) **Encouragement to Embrace the Unknown:**
The sermon concludes with an invitation to step into the unknown, trusting that God's plan will unfold in time. He emphasizes that blessings often come from unexpected directions, and only those willing to act without hesitation will witness the fullness of God's promise.

2. **The Biblical Quote and Its Interpretation**

a) **"Do Not Love the World or the Things in the World" (1 John 2:15):**
The biblical quote is central to the apostle's sermon. He explains that the world's temptations can draw believers away from God, making it essential to stay focused on spiritual matters.

b) **Separation from Material Desires:**
The apostle interprets the quote as a directive to detach from material possessions and purpose. He stresses that God's love and grace are far greater rewards than any earthly riches.

c) **Understanding the Context of Love in the Bible:**
The quote is explained in the context of God's unconditional love. The apostle explains that while worldly love is conditional and fleeting, God's love is eternal and unchanging.

d) **Application in Modern Life:**
The sermon draws parallels between the ancient biblical context and the modern believer's life. He warns against becoming overly attached to technology, money, or status, as these distract from one's relationship with God.

e) **Reassurance of God's Care for His Followers:**
Despite the warnings against worldly attachments, the apostle reassures the congregation that God's love will provide for all their needs, encouraging trust in divine provision over material pursuits.

3. **The Prophetic Message Delivered**

a) **The Call to Action:**
The apostle delivers a powerful prophetic message urging the congregation to act immediately on their divine calling. He proclaims that hesitation and doubt are hindrances placed by the enemy, and that stepping forward in faith is the only way to receive God's blessings.

b) **Promises of Divine Guidance:**
He speaks of a vision where God is guiding the people, and those who trust in Him will be led to places of abundance and spiritual fulfilment. The message is clear: God is already at work in their lives, and they must only follow.

c) **Blessings for the Obedient:**
The apostle declares that those who obey will see an increase in blessings—financially, spiritually, and emotionally. He assures them that God is opening doors and removing obstacles for those who trust and act on His word.

d) **Warnings for the Hesitant:**
The message includes a caution for those who delay or refuse to follow God's call. The apostle states that delaying obedience could result in missed opportunities and divine appointments.

e) **The Urgency of the Times:**
He emphasizes that the times are urgent, and the world is changing rapidly. The apostle encourages the congregation to act now, as the window for divine Favor is open. The message concludes with a prophetic assurance that God will meet them where they are if they move in faith.

4. Lessons for the Congregation

a) **Trusting God's Plan Over Personal Desires:**
The apostle teaches that trusting in God's plan, even when it conflicts with personal goals, is a key to spiritual growth. He encourages the congregation to surrender their own ambitions in Favor of God's will.

b) **Faith Without Action Is Empty:**
The apostle underscores the importance of taking action, saying that faith must be demonstrated through works. Believing in God's promises is only half of the journey—acting on that belief is what brings results.

c) **Living a Life of Service:**
The message emphasizes that each believer is called to serve others. Whether through ministry, charity, or kindness, serving is the way to align oneself with God's purpose.

d) **Overcoming Doubt Through Prayer:**
Doubts and fears are acknowledged as natural, but the apostle teaches that prayer can overcome these obstacles. By praying for strength, believers can move forward with confidence in God's plan.

e) **Building a Legacy of Faith:**
The apostle encourages the congregation to think beyond the present and consider the legacy of faith they are building. By acting in obedience and trust, they can leave a lasting impact on future generations.

Chapter 7 –

Time out Mission International World Conference London, UK

1. The Sermon Preached by the Apostle

a) **The Metaphor of the Boat:**
The apostle presents the journey of faith as a voyage across the lake, where believers must choose whether to stay on the shore, hang onto the boat, or enter fully into God's vessel. The boat represents God's calling, and entering it symbolizes complete faith and trust.

b) **Stages of Faith:**
The sermon divides believers into three categories: those who stand on the shore (watching), those hanging on to the boat (in indecision), and those inside the boat (fully committed). The apostle invites all to step inside the boat and embrace God's will fully.

c) **The Call to the Other Side:**
Drawing from the Gospel of Luke (Chapter 8:22), the apostle emphasizes Jesus' command to "go to the other side," encouraging believers to take action and move towards their divine purpose, even when obstacles seem overwhelming.

d) **The Storm and the Cry for Help:**
As the boat faces a storm, the disciples panic, crying out for help. The apostle parallels this to how modern believers react to challenges despite knowing that Christ is with them. He stresses the importance of remembering God's presence and promises during trials.

e) **Faith Amidst Fear:**
The apostle reminds the congregation that fear and doubt arise from a lack of faith. He challenges them to open their spiritual eyes, recognize God's power guiding the boat, and trust that they will safely reach the other side.

2. The Biblical Quote and Its Interpretation

a) **Luke 8:22 – "Let's Go to the Other Side of the Lake":**
The apostle bases his message on this quote, interpreting it as an invitation to move forward in faith, leaving behind comfort zones (the shore) and embracing the uncertainty of the journey towards God's plan.

b) **Discipleship and Obedience:**
The quote serves as a reminder of the disciples' immediate obedience to Jesus' command. The apostle encourages believers to be equally prompt in their response to God's call, trusting His direction even when the path seems unclear.

c) **The Significance of 'The Other Side':**
The apostle interprets "the other side" as a metaphor for growth, transformation, and fulfilling one's divine purpose. He stresses that God's plans often require stepping into unfamiliar territory, but the rewards are worth the leap of faith.

d) **Challenges on the Journey:**
The storm the disciples face on their way to the other side represents the trials and obstacles believers face in their walk with God. The apostle highlights the importance of maintaining faith through these challenges, knowing that Jesus is always present.

e) **Reassurance in God's Promise:**
The apostle reassures the congregation that just as Jesus was with the disciples in the storm, He is with them in their struggles. God's promise to take them to the other side guarantees that they will arrive, even if the journey is turbulent.

3. The Prophetic Message Delivered

a) An Urgent Call to Enter the Boat:
The prophetic message is clear: believers still standing on the shore must enter the boat now. The apostle warns that staying in a place of indecision or comfort will lead to missed opportunities for spiritual growth and divine fulfilment.

b) **Grace Already Given:**
The apostle proclaims that the grace to enter the boat has already been given. The problem is not a lack of grace but the failure to recognize and act upon it. Believers are urged to step into God's plan without hesitation.

c) **The Danger of Hesitation:**
For those hanging onto the boat without fully committing, the apostle warns of the dangers of indecision. He explains that by neither committing to faith nor retreating to the shore, these believers leave themselves vulnerable to spiritual failure.

d) **The Assurance of God's Presence:**
The prophetic message reassures believers that God is present in the boat with them, guiding their journey. The apostle encourages them to trust that, despite the storms they may face, God will deliver them safely to the other side.

e) **A Plea to Stop Doubting:**
The apostle challenges those inside the boat who continue to doubt and cry out in fear. He reminds them that Jesus is with them and that there is no need to panic. The prophetic message is one of encouragement: have faith, and trust the journey.

4. Lessons for the Congregation

a) **Commitment to God's Plan:**
The key lesson is the importance of fully committing to God's plan. Whether in times of peace or storms, believers are called to trust God's guidance, knowing that He has already set the course.

b) **Faith Over Fear:**
The apostle teaches that fear is natural but must not dominate the believer's journey. Through faith, the congregation is encouraged to overcome doubt and trust in God's power to lead them through difficult times.

c) **Recognizing God's Grace in Action:**
Believers are reminded to recognize the grace that has already been given to them. Instead of waiting for a sign or assurance, they are called to act on the grace they have received and move forward in their spiritual journey.

d) **The Importance of Spiritual Readiness:**
The congregation is urged to always be spiritually ready, just as the disciples had to be prepared to follow Jesus. This involves not just listening to the Word but acting on it with conviction.

e) **Trust in God's Timing:**
Finally, the apostle emphasizes the importance of trusting God's timing. While storms may come and go, the congregation is reminded that God's plan will unfold at the right time, and they will arrive at the destination He has prepared for them.

Chapter 8 –

14 April 2018 Kampala. Uganda.
Is your temple a den of robbers? Day 3

1. "Is Your Temple a Den of Robbers?" - Matthew 21:13

Contextual Explanation:
The title draws from Matthew 21:13, where Jesus declares, *"My house will be called a house of prayer, but you are making it a den of robbers."* This verse reflects Jesus' righteous anger as He clears the temple, which had become a marketplace instead of a sacred space for worship.
In this sermon, delivered in Kampala, Uganda, the focus shifts from the physical temple of Jesus' time to the spiritual temples of our bodies and lives. The preacher challenges believers to examine how worldly distractions and misaligned priorities have corrupted their relationship with God.

The Sacredness of the Temple:
The passage reminds us of the holiness of God's house and the need to honour it with prayer and reverence, both in physical churches and within ourselves as spiritual temples.

Confronting Worldly Distractions:
The "den of robbers" represents how materialism, greed, and sin can invade the sacred spaces of our lives. The preacher emphasizes the importance of clearing these distractions to make room for God's presence.

Call to Action:
Believers are urged to reflect on their lives and ask themselves, "Is my temple a house of prayer or a den of robbers?" This introspection forms the foundation of the chapter, urging a spiritual cleansing and a renewed commitment to God.

2. Sermon Preached

Personal Testimony:
The preacher shared experiences from their travels across the globe, observing how churches and individuals often prioritize worldly concerns over spiritual devotion. From bustling marketplaces outside churches to corrupted practices within, the testimony shed light on the universal struggle to maintain the sacredness of worship spaces.

Connection to the Cleansing of the Temple:
Drawing parallels to Jesus overturning tables in the temple, the preacher reflected on modern-day challenges faced by congregations. "When Jesus sees your temple, what will He find?" they asked, emphasizing the need for spiritual renewal.

The Role of the Holy Spirit:
The preacher reminded the congregation that the Holy Spirit is ready to dwell within them but can only do so when the temple is purified. "You are a temple of God," they declared, urging believers to clear out anything that hinders God's presence.

Encouragement to Take Action:
The sermon ended with a passionate call to clear the "tables" in our lives. Just as Jesus restored the sanctity of the temple, believers were encouraged to restore holiness in their own lives through repentance and prayer.

3. Biblical Quote: Matthew 21:13, "My house will be called a house of prayer, but you are making it a den of robbers."

Divine Instruction:
This verse highlights Jesus' demand for reverence in God's house, urging believers to prioritize prayer and worship over worldly distractions.

Faith in Action:
The passage serves as a call to actively remove anything that corrupts the sanctity of our spiritual lives. Just as Jesus physically cleansed the temple, believers must take action to cleanse their hearts and minds.

Transformation Through Purity:
The temple's cleansing symbolizes spiritual transformation, showing how purity paves the way for God's presence and blessings.

Application to Modern Life:
The verse challenges believers to evaluate their daily lives. Are we making space for God, or have we allowed worldly concerns to take over?

Manifestation of God's Glory:
When the temple was cleansed, the blind and lame entered and were healed by Jesus. This demonstrates that spiritual renewal opens the door for divine intervention and blessings.

4. Prophetic Message

Call to Faith:
The preacher delivered a prophetic message urging the congregation to purify their spiritual temples. "The Holy Spirit is ready to enter," they proclaimed, "but only if you make space for Him."

Victory Over Worldly Distractions:
The message emphasized the need to reject materialism, greed, and sin. "Throw out the robbers," the preacher declared, encouraging believers to take an uncompromising stance against anything that distracts from God.

Unity in Worship:
The congregation was reminded of the power of collective faith and prayer. Just as Jesus' actions united the temple under God's purpose, believers were called to come together in unity to restore the sacredness of worship spaces.

Encouragement for Spiritual Growth:
The prophetic words promised transformation and renewal for those who take the call seriously. "When you clear the temple, miracles will follow," the preacher assured, referring to the healings that occurred after Jesus cleansed the temple.

5. Reflection and Application

Personal Reflection:
Believers are encouraged to examine their lives and identify the "tables" that need to be overturned. Are there distractions, habits, or sins that have taken the place of prayer and devotion?

Acting on Faith:
The chapter emphasizes the importance of taking concrete steps to restore holiness. Whether it's dedicating more time to prayer or eliminating negative influences, believers are called to act in faith.

Restoring Sacredness:
Readers are reminded that their bodies are temples of the Holy Spirit. Keeping them pure and dedicated to God allows His presence to dwell within and work through them.

Transformation Through Obedience:
The act of cleansing the temple is both symbolic and practical. By removing distractions and focusing on God, believers can experience profound spiritual transformation.

Daily Application:

The chapter concludes with practical steps for maintaining spiritual purity: regular prayer, repentance, and seeking God's guidance in all aspects of life. By keeping their "temple" holy, believers can create space for God's presence and blessings.

Chapter 9 –

26 August 2022 Monday Service with Rev Dr Antony Walto at Dubai Emirates Accommodation and at Stefan Ark, Ernakulam (Malayalam Service) Divine Family Monday Service by Rev. Dr Antony Walto and son Shine Morais.

1. "Responding to God's Call" (26 August 2022, Monday Service)

- **The Power of Divine Invitation:** This title emphasizes the gospel message of Jesus calling His disciples, who are representing the divine invitation to serve Him and follow the path.

- **The Chosen Few:** Indicates how Jesus calls certain people for a purpose. The reader is challenged to consider if he or she is prepared to respond if God chooses him or her.

- **The Mountainside Symbolism:** The mountainside where Jesus called His disciples represents a place of solitude and spiritual elevation, a metaphor for where God invites His chosen ones to meet Him.

- **The Readiness to Answer the Call:** The title also calls on believers to consider their readiness. "Am I now ready to respond to Him spiritually when Jesus calls?

- **A Call to Ministry and Service:** The title is just a call to ministry and service, not a call of obedience to be followed but a call to be sent upon the world with an assignment and thus a reflection of discipleship.

2. **Sermon Preached**

- **Called for a Purpose:** The Reverend makes it known that the call of Jesus to twelve disciples on the side of the mountain signifies that God has a purpose in calling each individual He calls. It is not arbitrary but rather a divine choice.

- **The Response to the Call:** The sermon clearly puts forth that hearing God's call is an act and not just a hearer of the word; one can hear the call but not step out in faith and obedience for God to use him.

- **Authority and Mission:** The reverend explains that he who is called by the Lord is also empowered by Him. The twelve apostles were authorized to cast out demons and others were forbidden to do so, which revealed the fact that the call brings responsibility and divine power.

- **Facing Doubt and Rejection:** The message believes even Jesus faced the pains of scepticism and rejection.

The world does not always understand nor support the mission, but the call presses on with the strength that God gives.

- **Unity in the Call:** The apostle underscores the importance of unity among those called. For a divided house cannot stand, nor a divided church or community. This message is therefore a call to a common mission among believers under Christ.

3. **Biblical Quote: Mark 3:13 - "Jesus went up on a mountainside and called to him those he wanted, and they came to him."**

- **Jesus' Divine Selection:** The verse paints a vivid picture of the deliberate action Jesus made in choosing those whom he wanted to be close to him. As such, God has special plans with every single individual whom He calls.

- **Going to the Mountainside:** The mountainside is symbolic of a place where individuals are set apart to receive a higher purpose. It calls believers to separate themselves from distractions and seek God's presence.

- **Obedience to the Call:** Those called by Jesus responded promptly. The verse reminds the believers of the importance of obedience whenever they hear God's voice calling them.

- **Invitation to Intimacy with God:** The call of the disciples was not about following but being with Jesus. This emphasizes that relationship and intimacy with God are part of discipleship.

- **Empowerment for Mission:** The verse reminds that God never commissions without equipping. All such as find Him are commissioned to go out with power and authority to complete the mission of God on earth.

4. **Prophetic Message**

- **A Time to Reflect on Your Calling:** As part of the prophetic word, one calls people to reflect on whether they have, in fact, heard God's call and, also based on that call, whether they are living according to it. Are they living out the purpose for which they are called?

- **God's Call is Personal:** The message affirms that God's call is tailor-made for each individual. While Jesus chose His twelve disciples, so also does God single out every believer for a special assignment.

- **Preparation for Greater Works:** The prophetic message reassures believers that God is preparing them for bigger works. Just like the disciples were given authority, believers are empowered too for their work.

- **Facing Rejection with Faith:** The message reminds the believers that, like Jesus, they may encounter opposition or doubt the world. But they must not be discouraged because God's approval matters.

- **Empowerment Through the Holy Spirit:** The last message reminds the believers that the Holy Spirit equips them for the mission. They are not to venture out alone but with divine guidance and authority so that every hurdle can be tackled.

5. "Lessons on Spiritual Unity"

- **Unity in the Body of Christ:** The chapter was heavily underlined in areas where unity has to be brought about within the church as well as within the body of Christ. Division only serves to weaken the overall mission, whereas unity must indeed precipitate actual progress within God's Kingdom.

- **Division is a Threat to Spiritual Growth:** Division in any perspective, whether within the church or within the family, poses a danger to spiritual growth. As the Bible says, 'a house divided against itself cannot stand.' Neither can a church divided against itself stand. A church divided against itself loses its power and influence.

- **Strength in Togetherness:** Christians are encouraged to acknowledge their strength in unity. In this state, they can accomplish much more than if they were alone or divided by one's interests.

- **A Call to Reconcile Differences:** The chapter encourages believers to seek reconciliation as a necessity where division exists, whether family members or members within the church community. Through reconciliation, healing, and community strength are realized.

- **One Mission, One Purpose:** The last reminder of this chapter for believers is that all are working toward the same mission-to spread the gospel and to bring others to Christ. When they view themselves as working toward one common purpose, unity is accomplished.

Chapter 10 –

"Sermon of Public Meeting: Day 1, Kenya" - 25 May 2014

Contextual Explanation:
The title stems from Matthew 18:20, where Jesus assures His presence in the gathering of believers united in His name. This verse emphasizes the power and sanctity of fellowship, prayer, and collective faith.
The first public meeting held in Kenya on May 25, 2014, revolved around the importance of faith, unity, and recognizing Jesus' presence among His people. The preacher spoke passionately, encouraging the audience to open their hearts to God's word and reminding them that faith in action can bring about transformation.

The Power of Gathering in His Name:
Jesus' words highlight that wherever believers come together, God's presence is with them, making their prayers and worship more powerful. This truth sets the foundation for the sermon's focus on spiritual readiness and the power of collective faith.

Call to Recognize His Presence:
The preacher urged believers to attune their hearts to the divine presence and trust in God's power to transform their lives. The verse serves as a reminder that unity in faith can break barriers and pave the way for God's miracles.

Relevance in Modern Times:
Even today, the promise of Jesus' presence in the gatherings of His followers assures believers that God is always near, providing strength, guidance, and peace.

Sermon Preached

Personal Testimony:
The preacher shared insights from years of ministry, recounting moments when small gatherings of faithful believers experienced profound spiritual breakthroughs. These personal anecdotes illustrated how faith in collective prayer opens doors to divine intervention.

Connection to the Promise of Jesus' Presence:
Drawing from Matthew 18:20, the preacher emphasized that the power of any gathering lies not in its size but in its purpose. Whether two or two thousand gather, the presence of Jesus is promised when the focus remains on Him.

Faith and Unity:
The sermon highlighted the importance of unity in faith, drawing parallels between the congregation in Kenya and biblical examples of collective faith leading to miracles. The preacher encouraged the audience to support one another, just as the four friends in Mark 2:1-12 carried the paralyzed man to Jesus.

Encouragement to the Congregation:
The preacher called upon the attendees to believe in the transformative power of God's presence.

"Do not underestimate what happens when you gather in His name," they said. The sermon concluded with an appeal for spiritual readiness, urging the congregation to approach God with faith and humility.

Biblical Quote: Matthew 18:20, "For where two or three gather in my name, there am I with them."

Divine Assurance:
This verse provides believers with the assurance of God's presence, emphasizing the importance of community in faith.

Faith in Action:
The promise of Jesus' presence reminds us that faith is not an individual journey but a shared one. It encourages believers to come together in prayer and worship, trusting that God is with them.

Transformation through Unity:
When believers unite in His name, their collective faith can lead to spiritual transformation, healing, and breakthroughs.

Application to Modern Gatherings:
The verse challenges believers to prioritize meaningful fellowship and recognize the sanctity of every gathering centred around God.

Manifestation of God's Glory:
Through the collective faith of believers, God's power is revealed, demonstrating His ability to work through unity and devotion.

Prophetic Message

Call to Faith:
The preacher delivered a prophetic call to the congregation, urging them to embrace the promise of Jesus' presence. "You are not alone in this gathering," they declared. "Jesus is here, ready to move among you."

Victory through Unity:
The prophetic message emphasized the strength that comes from unity. The congregation was reminded that when believers stand together in faith, they can overcome any obstacle.

Encouragement to Seek God's Presence:
Believers were encouraged to approach God with humility and expectation, trusting that His presence would bring transformation and renewal.

Assurance of Grace and Guidance:
The preacher assured the congregation that Jesus' presence would guide them, providing clarity and strength in their spiritual journey.

Hope for the Future:
The prophetic words ended on a note of hope, promising

that God's blessings would follow those who gathered in His name with sincere hearts.

Reflection and Application

Personal Reflection:
Believers are encouraged to reflect on the state of their spiritual gatherings. Are they centred around Jesus, or have worldly distractions crept in?

Acting on Faith:
The chapter emphasizes the importance of actively participating in fellowship and prayer, trusting that God's presence will bring transformation.

Building Strong Communities:
Readers are reminded of the power of unity in faith. By supporting one another, believers can create communities that reflect God's love and purpose.

Transformation through Obedience:
The promise of Jesus' presence requires believers to approach gatherings with humility and devotion. By doing so, they can experience spiritual renewal and growth.

Application in Daily Life:
The chapter concludes with practical steps for fostering meaningful fellowship: regular participation in prayer meetings, building relationships within the faith community, and seeking God's presence in every aspect of life.

Dear Rev.Dr. Antony Walto,

Greetings from your brethren in Ghana to you in Jesus name. Am writing you this letter on behalf of King Of Kings bible college Ghana and oversea, Full Gospel Centre(church) Ghana, and Bishop Asante Outreach Ministries. You have ministered severally in our ministry and we have known you as a brother based on your gift and the holy spirit in you. The hands of God is upon you, you are humble and dynamic. This made us to recommend you to be awarded with doctorate degree in one of our programs in Ghana.

Having heard about your upcoming book, we were all glad in Ghana because we know what is in you and if you can document some in a book, it will benefit the whole world. Therefore I may also recommend this book to everybody who may like to improve in life, ministry and Christianity to get
some.

I believe this book will change lives everywhere and every time. May the good Lord bless you Rev. Dr. Antony Walto for the good works which you are doing to support the work of God.

Yours in Christ
Rev. Ephraim Henry Asante (Administrator)
KING OF KINGS WORLD FOUNDATION P.O.BOX A/T 1193, ACHIMOTA-ACCRA. GHANA
HEAD OFFICE, POKUASE, KATAPOR ESTATE

WEBSITE: www.kokwf.webs.com.
EMAIL: interbibleseminary@yahoo.com
TEL: +233 2436 76766/ +233 27615 5382

Introduction:

Carrying the Flame of Faith Across Nations

I am a Spirit filled Man of God given my life to our living Lord Almighty. This calling wasn't a casual choice; it is a burning desire, a passion that has led me to surrender everything to see God's purposes fulfilled in people's lives. That is born out of that calling and journey that God has taken me on to bring His message to people around the world.

The Righteous God has blessed me with such a journey and privilege in traveling across and across the continents and nations of the earth. His Good News with the people of United Kingdom, United States, Canada, Australia, New Zealand, Singapore, Malaysia, Uganda, Kenya, Zimbabwe, Ghana, Cameroon, Nigeria, South Africa, United Arab Emirates, India. Not once several times. In all these places, the power of the Holy Spirit had been dominant - asserting power in preaching, teaching, prophesying, Revelation, healing, and casting out demons. Every messages, every revelation, and every act of deliverance is a witness to God's presence as well as to His will to touch lives and cities through His Spirit.

This book traces a journey I have walked as a servant of His, from place to place, and in the lives of people marked by brokenness, fear, confusion, and doubt.

But in each meeting, the Holy Spirit has manifested to bring deliverance, healing, and hope. I have seen their lives turn around, even those bonds broken and strongholds fallen as God's power flows freely upon them. I love that as you read these words, the same Spirit who worked wonders in those meetings would stir within your spirit and bring you into the fulfilment of your God-given destiny.

I've walked with Him through many lands, faced different issues, and got an up-close look at the deep resistance that lies within the heart toward faith. But I have also seen enormous transformations when people open their ears and hearts to the work of the Spirit. It is my desire in this book to present again or to bring you along, an encounter through which I hope you will be stirred to continue deeper interaction with God, more sensitivity to the promptings of the Holy Spirit, and respond to His call with an attitude of faith and life surrendered to His purpose.

I would like the body of Christ to come to maturity, strength, and unity. That's my mission and that's the mission of this book. The greatest thing I could hope for, however, would be for the people of God to come into their faith strength, understanding who they are in Christ and what they have been called to do for His Kingdom. I want to see the Church be a perfectly aligned will of God and a great, moving, powerful body, all invigorated by the Holy Spirit, bringing light into dark corners, bringing truth in place of deception, and bringing freedom for the captive.

But to the reader of this book, I want to speak directly to your spirit: God has a purpose for your life. He has a plan for you, one that far surpasses your most incredible imagination. He yearns to see you walk in His power, authority, and wisdom. It is my prayer that in these chapters you will experience the presence of the Holy Spirit, be changed from the inside out, and come to know your part in God's great story.

So let us journey together with open hearts and expectant spirits. May the pages that follow give you encouragement, challenge, and inspiration that lead you into a deeper relationship with God and a greater sensitivity to His Spirit. He's the one we appeal to; he's the one we run to. The call is to his life and through his spirit in whom we are called, equipped, and empowered to do His will establish His purposes, and see His kingdom come on earth as it is in heaven. This book is an invitation to step into the fullness of God's plan for your life.

Dear Apostle Antony Walto,

Congratulations on the release of your new book! I am confident that it will be a tremendous blessing, not only to those who believe in Jesus Christ, but to everyone who cares to read it.

Since you spoke at our Kingdom Leadership Summit nearly a decade ago, the impact of your message has lingered on in my life and in the lives of all who heard you speak. Your words then, as they do now, continue to inspire and transform.

Over the years, we have closely followed the growth and global impact of your ministry, and it fills us with joy to see how God is using you to reach people worldwide.
This book is yet another testament to your dedication to God's work, and we celebrate it, knowing it will bear lasting fruit in the Kingdom of God and in the world at large.

We eagerly look forward to the testimonies that will come forth because of this book. To God be all the glory for your life, your family, and your ministry. May He continue to bless and expand your reach in the years to come.

With heartfelt congratulations and blessings,
Apostle Nosakhare Alex Ihama
Author, The Mystique of Leadership,
President/CEO, International School of Greatness
www.alexihama.com

Chapter 1 – 10 April 2022 United States Arlington GA, USA

"I tell you, get up, take your mat and go home." (Mark 2:11)

Take Your Mat and Go Home

I stand before you today to remind you of a message given to me, and I hope that I can share it with one and all who are ready to listen and open up their hearts. It is more than a meeting; it is a divine appointment for each of us, a moment to really understand the power behind Jesus' words in Mark 2:11: "I tell you, get up, take your mat, and go home."

Today, I ask you to imagine yourselves as that paralyzed man on that mat. The burden of dependence, struggles, and all those years, poured over in vain awaiting the moment. Then there stands, strong and resolute Jesus, calling you thus: "Get up! This is no ordinary call; it's a command layered with faith, a power that goes beyond the physical aspect, of the soul. The man lying there could not rely on his strength to move him; he based his movement on the faith of the people around him who believed Jesus healed.

And today, I urge you to do the same: to find strength in faith and the support of those around you. This is not just physical healing; it is far more profound. The mat symbolizes all those things we cling to out of habit—our past struggles, pain, and even our dependence on others for validation or strength. Jesus didn't heal him to be healed but free to stand up and walk and carry his testimony out into the world. And I believe that message still resonates with each one of us today.

It is a reminder that whenever He gives us His command, our role isn't to question or ponder but to respond in obedience with faith. Let's not forget that power was unleashed by those surrounding the man who lowered him down through the roof to get to Jesus. That wasn't an easy task; that's a labour of faith. They looked through the obstacles and took bold steps, knowing well that if they could bring him in front of Jesus, the transformation would follow. Their faith, combined with his, created the miracle. Who are you surrounded by today?

Are there people who will pick you up, hold you up, and bring you to Jesus even when it gets hard? That call of "pick up your mat" is a call of responsibility. He healed that man so he'd not just lie there, but could walk in dignity. And each of us has a mat to take up – be it a struggle, a fear, or a dependency. But remember, He has given us the strength to rise. Today I urge you, in His name, to rise; take up your mat; and step into the freedom he has granted you.

Go home, but not the way you went in - renewed, restored, and empowered by His word.

Sermon Preached by the Prophet

As I speak this word to you today, remember, that I am just a vessel; a servant of God's Word. The power and the message are not mine but come directly from Him, and it is my privilege to pass them on to you. I have travelled far, guided here for a purpose, with words that have been placed upon my heart to speak directly to each one of you. So listen not with your ears, but with your spirit, as these words are meant to stir something much deeper in you.

The message in Mark 2:11 is profound in truth: healing not only comes through the divine touch of Jesus but also through the unity and faith of those around us. At that moment, Jesus said to the paralyzed man, *"Take up your mat and walk,"* a command that can resonate with each of us in our journey of faith. As I stood there saying this message to people gathered around, I watched as this touched hearts the way mine was touched so long ago. I sense and can almost hear the spiritual response as if the Spirit moves through them. I have come before you today similarly to address you, then you might also feel the truth.

I will now explain what happens once faith becomes active. Think of a man on his mat. He is paralyzed. He cannot reach to Jesus himself. One man may feel sorry and try to help, but he soon finds himself unable to lift this man himself.

One cannot carry that burden alone. When I am speaking this truth, then I see that it roots itself, and here as well, it is urgent: one man may well be willing, but still, without support, it is impossible for him to bring this man out here. And so, another man cries out for friends. *He reaches out, and another man grasps the man's mattress.* Still, it lacks something. They need more, and soon a third comes, then a fourth, all united in purpose. When they come together with a common heart, bound by faith, they can lift the paralyzed man and carry him through the crowd, even climb to the top of the house and tear open the roof to lower him down before Jesus. They alone, with a common aim, can bring this man to the place of healing. *Four people with one heart, one faith—that is the power of unity in faith.*

But what if, of these four, one does not have faith? If one falters, if just one person doubts, the balance shifts, and the mat cannot be held. All the journey fails if all four do not carry equal faith. That is why I say that unity in belief, in conviction, is necessary. If you would like to help hold somebody up toward healing, then your faith must be steadfast, and your purpose with others united.

That day they in that room saw it, felt it, and many cried. It is to those that day that I speak to today: *faith is the door opening to the heavens and giving divine healing.* You can take someone carrying if you will in their hour of need - but you have to do so all the way, completely on trust. You cannot persuade, for you have to keep a steadfast heart and firm grip on that way to Jesus.

Only this way can you take those you love in His presence, to lay them down and say, "Here, Lord. We brought them to you. Heal them."

Biblical Quote: Mark 2:11 - "I tell you, get up, take your mat and go home."

The words of Mark 2:11: an absolute command—so simple, yet so overflowing with divine energy. Jesus looked at that paralyzed man, focusing directly on his deepest need. "Get up, take your mat and go home." These are words of authority, faith, and love. When Jesus speaks, it's not a suggestion; it is a command stirring within the very spirit, and touching something deep within. His words to the man reminded him that even the power that could create worlds had within itself the power to heal, transform, and renew.

This verse is very meaningful for us because more than healing the physical condition, Jesus speaks life and purpose into the man's soul. "Get up" wasn't just rising physically; it was a call to rise spiritually, emotionally, and mentally. It was a call to overcome every limitation that had defined this man. Many of us, at times, have felt paralyzed - not by illness, but by fear, doubt, or past wounds. However, just as the paralyzed man heard His voice calling him to "get up," it will remind us that His word would have broken through any barrier, therefore keeping us down.

When Jesus said, "Take your mat," He was giving him a job, a task. And the once-symbols-of-helplessness mat became a victory symbol. He wanted him to carry that mat to remind him of how far he had come. That mat was a transformation symbol, the proof of the journey from weakness into strength. Jesus wanted him never to forget whence he had come, but to take this forward as a testimony: every time he saw that mat, he remembered and everyone around him recalled God's strength in his life.

And finally, "go home." These are the words from Jesus, and it's not just about direction. They're about restoration. Jesus didn't send him to just any old place; He sent him home, back to his loved ones, back to the life that once seemed impossible. Healing is never just for us alone. When God works in our lives, it ripples out to those around us: our families, our friends, our communities. By sending him home, Jesus brings back this man to his family and community, bringing him back to his purpose. In Mark 2:11, Jesus' command writes a hope-filled message for all of us. Whomsoever we find ourselves with, at whatever has held us back, He speaks the same life-changing words to us: "Get up, take your mat, and go home." These words invite us to rise and carry our testimonies, and march boldly back into those lives we were designed for. It's like saying, Come to change, reminding us that with Him, there's a way back to hope, to purpose, and to wholeness.

Prophetic Message

The message I bring today is not for those reading words only but a personal call to each open heart to listen. This message digs into the very core by asking, "Where are you now?"—because wherever you are is where Jesus stands ready to meet you there. Just as He met the paralyzed man in Mark 2, He's waiting to help you get up, take your mat, and go forward with purpose.

I believe that to rise out of desperation a man needs faith, though not complicated or hard, but faith that comes out of an awfully simple movement of trust. Jesus called out to the man, "Rise." Can you imagine the depth that one little word has? When He calls us to rise, He asks us to stand up from that which has held us down. No matter how terrible your situation is, it is not beyond His reach. It's high time we rise from our circumstances, step out of helplessness into strength, out of hopelessness into faith. As you read these words, know this: the power to rise is yours because His voice spoke it into being.

He said, "Take up your mat."

The mat was what defined them in their worst place. This is where we have been confined, weighed down with burdens, places where we are limited. But when Jesus commands us to take it up, this mat becomes the embodiment of strength. It is no longer a symbol of suffering but now it is a symbol of victory; something you carry as a testimony of God's grace in your life.

Jesus was ordering the man to pick up his mat so the man could now go around proclaiming himself to the world that he had been healed. He says, "Do not forget where you came from. Do not hide your story. Pick up that mat and let it remind you of what I have done."

Jesus tells us not just to rise and carry our testimony but also to "go home." He sends us back into the lives we came from, yet we're no longer the same. The healing and freedom we receive are not for us alone but for all those around us. When Jesus healed this man He restored him not only physically but spiritually and socially, returning him home where he could live as a witness to those who knew him best. It does not get any better than it does when it touches others; our testimony shines brightest in the places we've been before.

Today, this prophetic message is one of deliverance and restoration. It is an invitation to the paralysis of our own hearts and in newness of life. Many are in situations where, despite their urge to advance ahead, they hang on the edge, not sure if they are ready to commit to stepping into the boat of faith. But remember this: Jesus calls each of us to walk fully in His grace, not halfway. He does not want to have us hang over the precipice, insecure and afraid; He wants us in the boat, completely trusting in Him. When we are in, there is no turning back. Just like the disciples who followed Jesus across the lake, we are called to face the storms with courage, knowing that He is on the journey with us.

This sermon today is also on the grace that we've been given. This is the grace he gives to us freely, yet how many times do we ignore it while being lost in our struggles? We cling onto fear, worry, and doubt all the while as He sits waiting for us to come to see the action of His grace. He's calling you to step out from where you have been stuck and to claim what He's already provided in deliverance. But the best part of the story is yet to come: do not waste it; step forward, and let His grace carry you to places you never thought possible.

Many of us also live with spiritual paralysis. It is not necessarily visible, but it exists in our lives: the inability to step into full trust in God's purpose. As Jesus calls to the man in need, He calls to you and me today- maybe for the first time to rise, stand in faith, and walk in freedom. His words are full of authority, with the power to break any chain, spiritual or physical. If He says it must be so, then so it must be. His words are better than encouragement-they hold the key to stepping out of any and every bondage.

This is not only a message of personal freedom but a call to community with purpose. When God restores us, it's so that we can then be a light to others. Faith, by the people around us, in some ways is part of what heals and transforms us. Indeed, the four men who carried the paralyzed man made possible his encounter with Jesus. We too must carry one another, reminding each other of God's power and encouraging one another in faith.

Let us listen today to Jesus, challenging each one of us: "Arise, get up. Do not let anything hold you back. Grab hold of your mat—do not be afraid of your story and let it speak of the work I did in your life. Go home, bringing that light into others." When we respond to His word, the effects spread beyond our personal lives; we immediately influence all those through whom we live.

May we as individuals respond to this invitation today step out of our places of doubt, fear, and hesitation carry our testimonies boldly, and live out our faith for others to see. And as we go, may our lives reflect the power of His love, transforming not just our own journeys but the world around us.

Lessons in Faith and Action

In the healing story of the paralyzed man, Jesus teaches us that faith is not merely believing but a commitment to an action, a leap into the unknown based on the power and trust in Jesus. Faith does not act passively; it compels us to act and even step forward when we cannot see a clear path. This lesson teaches us not to believe but to take part in God's work, just like the four friends who brought a paralyzed man to Jesus, not to be deterred by any obstacle. Their persistence to reach Jesus and break through barriers symbolizes the lengths faith will go to find healing and transformation.

Of all the things here, community - that strength when others are standing beside one in their faith.

We have each other's support and can do that to friends, such as those four did. We'll find ourselves lying there on that mat-we cannot continue on our own at times- and at other times, we're there to drag a friend into healing. Just like those friends, faith unites us because we support each other to overcome those problems for which we could not find solutions by ourselves.

Command to "take up your mat" teaches one that once healed then there is a responsibility to act. The Mat which has now symbolized limitation from one moment to now is a reminder of God's grace. This implies carrying the mat: this testimony that we are living today. We share our stories of going through such a phase and then turning out to be strong. Thus, the testimony encourages others. The testimony about the mat also informs us that dignity has been restored unto us through Jesus. He does not tell the man to walk only. He tells him to go home. The very command is a call toward normalcy, community, and resumption of life in abundance. The healing that comes from Jesus is supposed to restore us to our own purpose and wholeness so that we may continue to live and be good to others. Jesus' command is a call to live in such a way that honours the new life he has given us, so each day is an expression of gratitude and faith.

The last lesson we learn from this passage is perseverance. The friends of the paralyzed man faced a crowded room, but that did not stop them. Their faith was unrelenting, pushing through even when it entailed breaking through a roof to reach Jesus.

We are challenged to have such determination, to let nothing hold us back from seeking the healing and guidance of God. Faith often requires the persistence of a willingness to break through whatever stands in the way. This is a story that is calling us to stand up and stand with one another, boldly carry our testimony, and push forward with complete trust in Jesus, knowing that nothing is too hard for Him through these very acts.

SUN INNS
Main Host
BISHOP DR. JOH SEER &
1ST LADY DR. JAMIE SEER
HIGHLIGHTS: CONSECRATION, ORDINATION, LICENSING,
Its Apostolic, Prophetic, Pastoral, Evangelistic
Theme
HOLY GHOST
ENCOUNTER
DR. ANTHONY W
UAE Dubai
APOSTLE PATRICE Y
South Africa
PASTOR JOHNSON
Bangkok, Thailand
PROPHET N. B. NOAH
Cameroon
Ghana
Pst. S.N Kevin
Taiwan
For Enquiry contact +6010 291 6196 Email: apafederation@windowslive.com

ROYAL CHRISTIAN
EVANGELICAL MISSION
11th November 2024
Rev. Dr. Antony Walto!

Prophet Walto, | want to thank God for your life and the new thing the Lord is doing through
you at this end time.
From the day we met at Ghana, | have the witness in my Spirit that you are a prophet of God, couple with the gift of deliverance and working of miracles, you are also the man of the Word.
Hearing about the publication of your book | give God the praise , because this generation need to share from the blessings that God have deposited in you.
On behalf of my ministry Royal Christian Evangelical Mission Lagos Nigeria, We know that you will reach, touch, and change many people through this book.
God bless you on your continued and growing global outreach!

Yours in Christ,
Apostle Dr. Amos Akinwale
General Overseer
Apostle Dr.
Royal Christian Evangelical Mission
Lagos Nigeria
3a Okojevoh street, by Olufarinda street, via Y/S street, Itire Bus stop, llogbo, Ajangbadi, Ojo, Lagos, Nigeria.
E-mail:rochrivent@gmail.com ,
rochemyouth@yahoo.com.,
Phone: 08023715956, 08029633144, 08106885039

Chapter 2 –

21 Sept 2016 Sarpeman, Ghana

"They need not go, you give them something to eat" (Matthew 14:16)

You Give Them Something to Eat

As I stood before the congregation that day in Sarpeman, Ghana, the scripture Matthew 14:16 echoed deeply within me: *"They need not go away; you give them something to eat."* It was more than an instruction from Jesus to His disciples—it was a direct call to each one of us, a challenge to step out in faith and compassion, trusting God to work through what we have.

I want you to imagine being among those disciples, standing in a desolate place, surrounded by thousands of hungry people, and hearing Jesus say, "You give them something to eat." What must they have felt? Helplessness? Fear? Doubt? They looked at the limited resources in their hands—five loaves and two fish—and likely thought, *This is impossible!* Yet, Jesus wasn't testing their ability; He was testing their faith and willingness to trust Him.

The miracle of the feeding of the five thousand wasn't just about satisfying physical hunger. It was about demonstrating the boundless provision of God and the necessity of stepping into the unknown with faith.
It was about teaching the disciples—and us—that when we surrender what little we have to Him, He can multiply it in ways we could never imagine.

Today, I urge you to think about the areas in your life where God might be saying, *"You give them something to eat."* It may not be about food. It might be your time, your love, your talents, or your faith. The world around us is full of spiritual and emotional hunger, and Jesus is calling us to respond, not from a place of abundance, but from a place of obedience and trust.

The instruction Jesus gave wasn't just about meeting the immediate need of the crowd. It was an invitation for the disciples to participate in His divine work. He could have called down manna from heaven or fed the people Himself, but instead, He chose to involve His followers. In the same way, He chooses to work through us today. He asks for what we have, no matter how small or insufficient it may seem, and when we place it in His hands, He multiplies it.

This chapter is not just about a historical event; it is about a divine principle that is still alive and active. Jesus, the Bread of Life, is inviting us to be part of His mission to feed the hungry—physically, emotionally, and spiritually. He reminds us that the miracle begins not with what we lack but with what we have.

Are you willing to offer what's in your hands, no matter how small, and trust Him to multiply it?

Sermon Preached by the Prophet

As I delivered this message, my heart was filled with urgency and love for the people gathered. I spoke about the faith required to act in times of scarcity. Imagine the disciples standing there, holding only five loaves and two fish, surrounded by thousands of hungry people. What they had seemed laughably insufficient. Yet, Jesus instructed them to offer it anyway. He didn't ask for what they didn't have; He asked for what they did.

I reminded the congregation that faith isn't just about believing—it's about taking action, even when the odds seem stacked against you. The disciples obeyed, and that obedience set the stage for the miracle. Jesus took what they gave, blessed it, and multiplied it to feed everyone, with leftovers to spare. Isn't that the kind of God we serve? A God who not only meets our needs but exceeds them?

Compassion was at the heart of this miracle. Jesus saw the crowd and was moved by their hunger. He could have sent them away to fend for themselves, but His love wouldn't allow it. Instead, He turned to His disciples and said, "You give them something to eat." It was a call to action, a challenge to look beyond their limitations and trust in His provision.

I shared with them that this wasn't just a lesson for the disciples; it's a lesson for us. Each one of us has something to offer, no matter how small it may seem.

When we bring our gifts, talents, and resources to God, He uses them to accomplish His purposes. But it starts with obedience. The disciples could have hesitated or argued, but instead, they chose to trust Jesus. And through their trust, a miracle unfolded.

I also spoke about the power of unity in faith. The disciples worked together, distributing the food among the crowd. Their collective effort, combined with Jesus' blessing, created a ripple effect that satisfied thousands. This is a reminder for us as believers to work together in faith and purpose, trusting that God will use our unity to achieve His mission.

The sermon ended with a call to action: to live lives marked by compassion, faith, and obedience. I encouraged the congregation to step out of their comfort zones, to see the needs around them, and to trust that God will provide as they respond in faith. The message was clear: when we place what we have in God's hands, He will use it to do far more than we could ever imagine.

Biblical Quote: Matthew 14:16 –
"You give them something to eat."

This verse is a profound challenge to every believer. Jesus' words test our faith, push us out of our comfort zones, and call us to act with compassion and trust. When He said, "You give them something to eat," He wasn't asking the disciples to perform a miracle; He was asking them to trust Him to perform one through their obedience. The disciples' initial reaction—pointing out their lack of resources—mirrors how we often respond to challenges. We focus on what we lack instead of what we have. Yet, Jesus wasn't concerned with their limitations. He knew that the five loaves and two fish were more than enough in His hands.

This passage reminds us that God's resources are limitless. What seems impossible to us is entirely possible with Him. It calls us to shift our perspective from scarcity to abundance, trusting that God can multiply even the smallest offering.

At its core, this verse is a call to compassion. Jesus saw the hunger of the crowd and was moved to act. His instruction to the disciples wasn't just about providing food; it was about teaching them to care for others as He did. It was about showing them—and us—that love in action is a reflection of God's heart.

Finally, this verse points to a greater truth: Jesus, the Bread of Life, offers nourishment that goes beyond physical food. He satisfies the deepest hunger of our souls, providing eternal sustenance and hope. When we respond to His call with faith and obedience, we not only meet the needs of others but also experience the fullness of His grace in our own lives.

27th November 2024
Dear Dr Antony Walto,

Congratulations to you on your impactful ministry and the release of your new book on the Christian faith! This profound work illuminates our identity and purpose in Christ, inspiring believers to walk in their divine calling. A must-read for those seeking spiritual growth and fulfilment! I endorse this book and encourage everyone with a genuine heart for the Lord and His purposes to read it. It will be an invaluable resource for fulfilling God's purpose in your life and ministry and for advancing His Kingdom. Thank you, Dr Antony, for continually inspiring us to pursue a more excellent way.

Yours in God's Kingdom,
Apostle Israel Onoriobe
World Vision Crusade Outreach Ministries
Cape Town, South Africa
Web: wvcom-international.org

Chapter 3 –

27 OCT 2013. Zimbabwe E.F.M.I. Eternal Freedom Ministries International

SIGNS & WONDERS SUMMER SESSIONS.

"Then said Jesus unto the twelve, Will ye also go away?" John 6:67

Sermon by the Prophet

Today, I want to begin with a message based on the joy of worship. The Bible tells us that praise and worship are not just actions, but ways of drawing near to God, and experiencing Him firsthand. Let me ask you, are you ready to feel God's presence today? Are you ready to let His Spirit fill you with gifts, peace, and purpose?
The sermon begins with a great call to worship, reminding us how great praise is in every believer's life. Hallelujah! With every "Hallelujah!" and every song we sing, we connect to His love, grace, and promises. We are singing not just to sing; we are opening a conduit for His Spirit to be active within us.

Thus, the Holy Spirit is also a gift to us who guide us, helps, and fills us with supernaturally gifted gifts. Examples include prophecy, wisdom, healing, and speaking in tongues, gifts that are indeed supernatural, beyond human ways and abilities. They act as tools that God puts within us to strengthen our faith, help others out there, and be more like vessels for His working. You might ask why God would give such gifts. The answer is simple: He loves us, and through these gifts, He equips us to live out His purpose and reflect His glory.

Each one of us is uniquely gifted, and each gift serves a purpose in the lives of believers. God has planned well; there is wisdom in it, a purpose in every spiritual gift, and a blessing in every act of faith. The apostle, in this sermon, explains that our faith is the foundation for these gifts. When we stand firm in our belief, even when we don't yet see the answers, we are preparing ourselves to receive God's blessings.

Let's see the depth of what praise and connection with God means as we gather in worship. This is not routine; it's a divine encounter.

The "Hallelujah" we say is not just a word; it's a declaration of our faith, a testimony to God's enduring goodness, and open invitation to His presence dwelling among us. Hallelujah! We lift up our voices to shake the heavens. And as we lift our voices, we draw down His Spirit to rest upon us.

Ready to feel His presence? To let His Spirit flood every place in your life, change you from the inside out? Worship, my friends, is a powerful life-changing experience. The more we involve God in our worship, the more we give space to His Spirit for pouring upon us blessings, guidance, and divine gifts.

The Holy Spirit is an abstract concept, but what it means is God breathed living in us. He equips us, gives us knowledge, and empowers people to move mountains in faith; He grants supernatural gifts when we receive the Holy Spirit. The gifts surpass the human level to which one can aspire while on earth. Some include prophecy, wisdom, healing, and speaking different languages, and they cannot be solely for our gains. They are to be shared to lift those around us and to shine as a beacon of His love. Why does God have such gifts for us? Well, the answer's very simple, yet remarkably profound: He loves each of you. You are God's beloved, God's very own. And all of these spiritual gifts we find in Roman 12 enable us to do more of God's work by demonstrating His goodness and God's power. What if that were a gift personally crafted by God just for you to fulfil His special divine purpose.?

So let me remind you, that gifts are not done by chance but by choice. Each one of us has been given a specific gift and a call. And so, like each body part with its task, do we have our role in the body of Christ? For instance, some people are called to speak wisdom, those who have healing, while others will be called to the mysteries of God. This is very beautiful-to be diversified. Together we make the complete body of Christ.

So, by our different and unique gifts, we mirror love and grace to this world around us.

All of these gifts are indeed rooted in faith. Faith is like that soil through which such talents grow up. In all such acts of trusting the Lord without seeing some clear-cut visible answers before their eyes, they are in essence setting a stage for something miraculous to take place in our lives. Not easy to hold on, when we seem to get nothing out of our prayers, but patience is a virtue that faith requires. God sees every moment of waiting, every prayer, every small step of obedience. And He rewards those in His perfect timing who held fast to their faith.

Let us open our hearts wide to Him now. Release all your fears, doubts, and uncertainties, and receive all the loving gifts He prepared for you. These are not for our glory but for His. Through us, God's love touches lives, heals the broken, and reaches those who feel far from Him.

Now take some time and ask the Lord what God has given you. What special talent He placed within you, so how could you employ this in making others know the Savior more intimately?

Accept that gift of God, depend on God's plan for your life, and follow Him's lead. For we have the calling from above; then His name is exalted through that call. Hallelujah!

Biblical Quote Explanation

As we explore these verses, let's take a moment to truly hear the voice of Jesus speaking to us, as though He were here with us right now. Each of these passages holds a powerful message, a call to deepen our faith and walk in alignment with His Spirit. Let's dive deeper into these verses and understand what they mean for us today, here and now.

Starting with **John 6:67:** "Then said Jesus unto the twelve, Will ye also go away?" This question is as relevant today as it was over two thousand years ago. Imagine Jesus looking into your eyes, asking you personally, "Will you also go away?" He's acknowledging that His teachings may sometimes be difficult to grasp, and that His path isn't always the easiest. But He wants to know who among us will remain steadfast. Life, my friends, isn't always smooth. We face trials, moments of doubt, and times when God's plan seems unclear. And it's in those moments that Jesus' question echoes: "Will you also go away?" It's a challenge, a call to make a conscious choice. Jesus isn't forcing us; He's inviting us. Our response reflects our commitment.

Just as the disciples chose to stay, trusting in Jesus despite their uncertainties, so are we called to stay faithful, even when life's circumstances don't make sense. Are you ready to answer His call and remain with Him, no matter what?

Now, **Acts 2:4** speaks to the day of Pentecost, a powerful day in Christian history when the disciples were "all filled with the Holy Spirit and began to speak with other tongues." The arrival of the Holy Spirit transformed ordinary people into vessels of God's extraordinary power. Speaking in tongues, a divine manifestation, was just one expression of God's presence within them. But let's consider the broader meaning here. When the Holy Spirit comes upon us, He brings with Him a deep transformation. He fills us with courage, wisdom, and strength that surpasses human understanding. With the Spirit's guidance, we become capable of things we never imagined. Imagine the Spirit flowing through you, empowering you to share God's love and message with everyone around you, to go beyond your limitations and doubts. This is what God promises each of us—that through the Holy Spirit, we are never alone, and that we are fully equipped to carry out His work.

Moving to **1 Corinthians 12:5-11**, we find a beautiful description of the spiritual gifts given to believers: wisdom, knowledge, faith, healing, prophecy, discernment, and more. These gifts are not random; each one serves a distinct purpose in God's kingdom. Some of us may be blessed with the gift of wisdom, guiding those around us.

Others may have the gift of healing, bringing physical or emotional restoration to the suffering. And still others may be gifted with prophecy, able to speak truth into people's lives. Every gift is a tool, meant to build up the church and the community.

God's gifts aren't about elevating ourselves; they're about lifting others up and showing love, compassion, and guidance. In sharing these gifts, we become instruments of God's work, shining His light into the world. Reflect on the gifts God has placed in you. How can you use them to serve others, to show His love, and to bring hope to those in need?

Matthew 6:1 gives us a powerful reminder: "Take heed that ye do not your alms before men, to be seen of them." Jesus is teaching us here about the purity of intention. When we do good, it should be done from a place of love, not for recognition. Jesus sees beyond the surface; He looks into our hearts. Imagine doing a kind act, helping someone, or giving generously—but without needing anyone to notice. This is true faith, true humility. God sees every hidden act of kindness, every moment of compassion, and every gift given in secret. And He treasures them. Jesus is asking us to examine our motives. Are we doing good to be seen, or are we doing it because it aligns with God's love? Let's commit today to serve quietly, to let our actions be a reflection of His love, and to trust that God sees and values everything we do in His name.

Finally, we come to **Mark 10:46-52,** the story of Bartimaeus, a blind man who persistently calls out to Jesus. Despite being told to keep quiet, Bartimaeus refuses to be silenced. His words ring out: "Jesus, Son of David, have mercy on me!" And Jesus hears him. He stops, listens, and heals him, saying, "Your faith has made you well."

What a powerful testimony of faith! Bartimaeus didn't let the voices of doubt or the people around him discourage him. He had one goal in mind: to reach Jesus. His story is a reminder that our faith must be persistent. We, too, may face voices that try to discourage us, and circumstances that make us doubt. But if we continue calling out to Jesus, if we stay steadfast in our faith, He will answer. Jesus is always ready to hear our cries, to meet us in our place of need. Today, let Bartimaeus's faith inspire you. Keep calling out, keep believing, and know that Jesus is listening.

As we reflect on these verses, let us remember that Jesus' words and actions are not just stories of the past—they are living truths that apply to us today. Jesus asks us to commit to Him, to remain faithful even in uncertainty. He offers us the Holy Spirit to empower us and reminds us to serve with humility. And, like Bartimaeus, He encourages us to approach Him with unwavering faith, trusting that He will respond. Let these verses resonate in your heart as you go forward, carrying the assurance that God is with you, equipping you, guiding you, and hearing your every prayer.

Prophetic Message

Today, I am called to bring you a message of hope and transformation. Even just as the apostles were filled with the Holy Spirit on the day of Pentecost, that same power is available to each one of us today. God's Spirit is here, reaching out, calling us to open up to receive His full presence.

He is calling us by name to open up our hearts and be filled with His Spirit. Imagine the power of this moment—a divine encounter, a time to set all distractions aside and listen for His call. This month I believe with all my heart will be one of breakthrough and blessing for those ready to receive.

I speak of a special anointing of healing—one that goes far beyond physical wellness. We tend to limit healing only to the body, but God's gift of healing touches every area of our lives. It is a healing of relationships, healing our inner wounds, those hidden places that need His touch. God's healing covers all of our fears, doubts, and every hurt we've carried. He is here to mend the broken places within us, to bring wholeness where there is brokenness. Imagine, for a moment, every part of you made whole, lifted up, restored. That is the promise of God's healing.

This message of healing is not only for us to receive but also to share. God's gifts are meant to flow through us to bless others. Think about what it would mean for each one of us to carry this gift of healing into the world. Visualize yourself as a vessel of God's love walking into spaces that need His peace and grace.

Visualize offering words of comfort to someone struggling or praying with someone who feels alone and discouraged. We prepare our hearts to believe this is not only possible but possible now. This is the time we step forward without doubts into faith because we know He wants to work through us.

God does not call us only receivers of His Spirit but also to be His ambassadors. But filled with the Holy Spirit it doesn't end with us. It overflows; it spreads out to those around us, lighting the darkest corners. This is a call to go beyond ourselves, letting the power of God's Spirit flow through us to transform not just our hearts but the lives that touch ours. It encourages us to be bold with the divine gift and to be a life that testifies to God's grace.

In this month of blessings, God is preparing us for something greater. We are called to carry His Spirit into the world, not timidly but boldly. Imagine if each of us was serious about this call. Just imagine if we were to live through that. How much change it would bring into our families, our communities, and even at our workplaces. If we have the light of the Holy Spirit in us, it illuminates us that we become sources of hope for each other and to remind each other of His love and power. It's no longer about wandering; we are part of something greater—a cause bigger than ourselves: unveiling glory for God before the world.

Then prepare yourself for this divine call. Take time to drop all the weight. Throw open your heart without restriction and ask God to fill you with His Spirit.
This month, when we open ourselves up to anointing by Him, we shall discover that gifts are not only in plenty but transforming. Allow change, healing, and restoration. Let God's Spirit move in you and through you and touch all about you.

The prophet here apostle Paul speaks plain and simple: God is moving his Spirit; therefore, he is calling His children, each of whom should participate in this effort. He is calling all to become His hands, to bring healing, and loving to this world, full of aching hurts which need all this healing from God. It is not a time to backpedal but rather to take a step forward. Let us be full of faith and see what God shall do through us. Accept this call each, understanding that we are not left alone in doing this God's Spirit goes along to empower us step by step.

Worship Experience

Worship, my friends, is far beyond a song or an assembly ritual. Worship is the celebration of joy, freedom, and unity with our heavenly Father. It is time set apart as a people joined together in one body - voices, hearts, souls, all being raised up to God to celebrate goodness and receive blessing. That worship brings us into an intimate relationship with God where we are laying aside every worry and every burden to surrender entirely to His presence. It is a celebration, in itself, an invitation to an encounter with God personally; a feeling of love, of grace, and guiding hands in life.

Imagine that mighty scene when we all come together, as the apostle calls us to let go, to sing without restraint, to dance with joy, and to praise with all our hearts. When we raise our hands, lifting them high in surrender, and our voices echo "Hallelujah" with every ounce of strength, we are not making noise.

We open the heavens to the spiritual world so that the Holy Spirit comes in and moves around us until He fills us. These are not invitations to glib worship but an appeal to celebration, freedom by God's presence, or communion with the very well of our Creator's soul.

The apostle challenges us to worship fully with complete joy and freedom. Imagine if all people, both children and the elderly, felt compelled to praise. Any song, any dance, any clap was a kind of faith declaration, announcing that we are here, we are His, and we trust in His goodness. Worship is letting go of whatever, in its place, allows His peace, joy, and strength to flood our lives. It's a time when our souls find freedom when everything else pales to insignificance, and we stand as His beloved, redeemed, and renewed.

In those moments of worship, something miraculous happens. Worship becomes a prophetic act, a time when God speaks to His people. Have you ever felt that pull, that voice in your heart, nudging you, guiding you during worship? It's in these times, as we collectively lift our praises, that God reveals His prophetic messages. He gives us direction, offering words of comfort, reassurance, and hope.

We receive the gift of divine connection through worship, the sense that He speaks directly to us, that He tells us to go on, hold on, and believe. In each song and prayer, we find His voice, and in His voice, we find our purpose.

Worship is not only a moment of receiving His messages but also a time of healing. The apostle talks of God's healing touch as a reality for each of us. So when we sing "Hallelujah," it is more than the word; it becomes a call to the Holy Spirit to come and heal from inside. Imagine God stretching his hand to mend that which is broken in our hearts, to restore weary souls, to touch that area which we did not think needed healing. Whether it be in emotional, physical, or spirit battles, God has this healing for you: not just a note of change, a lyric change, and a moment of praise- but that the Spirit and the Power are among the souls, infusing air for life into them as to renew strength, but reminded that with him anything is possible. Well then, let's have one of the most potent, tremendous releases through worship: setting me free from all of the stuff I may have inside. It frees us from our strife, insecurities, fears, and doubts. It's a way into growth - letting go of things no longer serving to receive that new life from God for us. Time to come vulnerable before him, time to lay aside our pride, and have him receive us in love to change us. When we worship, we say, "God, I am yours, completely. Do with me as you please." And in the act of surrender, lies freedom: from the sting of past hurts, from all fears about the future, and from all that grieves us.

In the act of worship, we unite ourselves also. In this stance shoulder to shoulder with fellow men praising God we are reminded we do not stand alone. We are part of a greater family, a community of believers united by faith, hope, and love. We lift each other and strengthen the body of Christ.

When we worship, we become one voice, one spirit, and one heart. There is beauty in knowing that regardless of the background from which we may come, we are linked together by His love and are encouraged and supported by one another through each other's faith. Worship reminds us that we are stronger as one unit, that united we can climb higher and, as one, bring to the world the loving nature of God.

As we worship, let's celebrate the spirit of unity and celebration with each other. Let us sing joyously, dance with bold abandon, and shout His name with irrepressible thanks. For at those moments, God is there among us. He is guiding, He is blessing, and filling us with His Holy Spirit. Each "Hallelujah" gets us closer to Him; our hearts are open farther to receive His grace in store for us. It is within these happy praises we sense His presence most deeply that we feel the power and love of Him in ways beyond our ability to speak or communicate.

And as we close our time of worship, let us recall that worship is not only for this moment. Worship is for every moment of our lives. Worship is a choice to walk every day of life living according to the heart He gave, walking with gladness, believing in what He says is going to be, and filling your heart with a thankful attitude.

One does not have to go to church to worship; one can worship anywhere, anytime. We can carry His joy with us; at work, at home, or even when we're alone with God in quiet moments. This is the heart of faith—living a life of worship, constant praise, constant gratitude, and an unshakable hope in His promises.

Let us carry this experience of worship with us today, let it echo in our hearts and minds. Let it inspire us to be light for others, to walk in His love, and to live every day in worship. For worship is not a song or a dance; it's a lifestyle- a daily expression of our love for God. Let it be our prayer, purpose, and pursuit.

CITIZENS'

Reverend Dr Antony Walto,

A Spirit filled man with a clear passion for the exertion for the living God. It is my prayer that this book which tells his Lord's heavenly story, will inspire you towards adventures in faith.
That you will yield to the anointing of the Holy Spirit who will lead you to be all that you can be, and to do all that you can do, through His work in your life.

With every blessing in Christ Jesus our Lord.
Archbishop Metropolitan Steven Evans
The International Christian Church Network
www.ticcn.org

Chapter 4 –

"Cast Your Net: Reflections on Manifestation of the Holy Spirit and Faith" - Jul 26, 2016, South Africa

"Be Ready to Receive It" - John 14:26

I stand before you with the words of Jesus in John 14:26 ringing in my heart: "But the Advocate, the Holy Spirit, whom the Father will send in my name, will teach you all things and will remind you of everything I have said to you." This promise is more than a verse; it is the cornerstone of our faith, a living truth that shapes how we walk with God daily. Today, I urge you, my dear brothers and sisters, to prepare yourselves—not just to hear, but to truly receive what God has in store for you. Are you ready to receive it?

As I stood before the congregation that day in South Africa, I could feel the Spirit moving even before the first word left my lips. The air was thick with expectancy, as if every heart in the room was waiting, yearning, and longing for something greater than what they had known before. It was not just a gathering; it was a divine appointment. And in that moment, I knew that the message I carried was not mine but His—a call to cast the nets of faith wide and deep, to trust in the abundance that God promises to those who believe.

The Holy Spirit is our Advocate, our Counsellor, and our ever-present help. But for Him to work in our lives, we must be ready to receive Him. And being ready requires more than mere willingness; it demands preparation. Imagine a fisherman casting his net into the sea. He does not see the fish; he has no guarantee of the catch. Yet he casts his net with faith, trusting that the unseen will become visible. That net, my friends, is faith. And the act of casting it is obedience.

I asked the congregation that day, "Where is your net? Have you cast it out, or are you holding it tightly in fear, afraid that it might come back empty?" Faith is not about certainty; it is about trust. It is about believing that when God says He will fill your net, He will do it—not in your timing, not according to your expectations, but according to His perfect will.

As the Word of God flowed through me, something extraordinary began to happen.
I saw tears streaming down faces, hands lifted high in surrender, and hearts breaking open to the Spirit's call. There were shouts of joy, cries of repentance, and whispers of gratitude. The Holy Spirit was moving, reminding each person of the promises of Jesus, teaching them to trust in His Word, and filling the room with His undeniable presence.

I told them, "Do not limit God by your doubts. Do not hold back your net because of past disappointments. If you do not cast it, how can it be filled?"

In that moment, the Spirit reminded me of a profound truth: God's blessings are not limited by our circumstances but by our readiness to receive. He is ready to pour out His Spirit, to teach us all things, and to remind us of everything Jesus has said—but we must be ready.

The net of faith requires strength, perseverance, and above all, trust. It is not enough to believe in God; you must act on that belief. Just as the fisherman prepares his net before going out to sea, so must we prepare our hearts. Are there knots in your net—knots of fear, doubt, or unforgiveness? Are there holes where faith has worn thin, where past hurts have torn through your trust? Bring them before the Lord. Let Him mend your net, strengthen it, and prepare it for the abundance He has promised.

I recall a woman from that congregation who approached me after the service, her face radiant with a joy she could barely contain. She said, "Pastor, for years I held onto bitterness and doubt, thinking that God had forgotten me. But today, when you spoke about casting the net, something broke inside me. I let go of my fear, and I felt the Holy Spirit fill me in a way I never thought possible." Her story is not unique. It is the story of all who dare to believe, who dare to cast their net even when the waters seem empty. The Holy Spirit is always ready, always willing, always present. He is the Advocate sent by the Father in Jesus' name to guide us, to teach us, and to remind us of His promises. But He cannot fill a net that has not been cast.

As the service continued, the Spirit's presence became almost tangible. People were falling to their knees, crying out to God, and experiencing breakthroughs they had long prayed for. It was a reminder to me, as much as to them, that the power of faith is not in its size but in its focus. Jesus said that even faith as small as a mustard seed can move mountains. But that seed must be planted; it must be nurtured.

Jesus' words in John 14:26 are a call to action. The Holy Spirit is here to teach us, to guide us, and to remind us of everything Jesus has spoken. But we must be willing to listen, to learn, and to remember. We must be willing to step out in faith, to cast our nets, and to trust that He will provide.

As I closed the sermon that day, I looked out at the faces before me—some tear-streaked, some smiling, all touched by the Spirit in some way. I said, "Do not leave here the same way you came. Take this message with you. Let it change you. Let it challenge you. And most of all, let it prepare you to receive the fullness of what God has for you."

Today, I say the same to you. Be ready to receive it. Let go of the doubts, the fears, and the failures that have held you back. Open your heart to the Advocate, the Holy Spirit, whom the Father has sent in Jesus' name. Let Him teach you, guide you, and remind you of the promises that are yours in Christ.

Cast your net wide, my friends. Trust that God will fill it with more than you can ask, think, or imagine. And when He does, be ready to receive it. For the Advocate is here, and He is ready to work in you, through you, and for you.

Sermon Preached

As I stood before the congregation, I could feel the weight of the message God had placed on my heart. It was not just a word for the people in the room; it was a divine mandate for every believer ready to step into the fullness of what God had prepared. This wasn't just about hearing the Word—it was about embracing it, living it, and acting on it. And so, I spoke from a place of both personal testimony and prophetic urgency, urging everyone present to cast their net of faith wide and deep.

I began by sharing a chapter from my own life—a time of struggle when the horizon seemed dark, and the answers to my prayers felt far away.
I had come to a place where my plans, my strength, and my efforts were no longer enough. It was in that moment of surrender, when I laid my plans before God and said, "Lord, I trust You," that the tide began to turn. It wasn't instant, and it wasn't easy, but it was transformative. Trusting in God's timing became the cornerstone of my faith, and through that trust, I experienced the power of divine provision.

I shared this testimony because I wanted the congregation to understand that God's plan is often beyond our comprehension.

It requires us to let go of what we think we need and to open our hearts to what He is preparing for us. I asked them, "Have you ever felt like you're casting your net into an empty sea? Have you ever wondered if your faith will truly bring you the blessings you seek?" These questions weren't rhetorical—they were an invitation for everyone to reflect on their own journey of faith.

The net became the central metaphor of the sermon, a symbol of both divine provision and human responsibility. I explained that the net represents our faith, our willingness to trust God and to act on that trust. But here's the catch: the size of the blessings we receive is often proportional to the size of the net we cast. The Lord spoke clearly to my heart as I prepared this message: "I am going to give you a larger net." But a larger net requires greater faith. It requires patience, perseverance, and the courage to cast it into the unknown, trusting that God will fill it in His perfect timing.
I looked out at the faces before me and said, "How large is your net? Are you casting it with confidence, or are you holding it back, afraid it might come back empty?" Faith, I reminded them, is not about certainty—it's about trust. It's about believing in God's provision, even when you can't see the blessings yet. It's about letting go of fear and doubt, and stepping boldly into the waters of His promise.
As the sermon unfolded, the Spirit began to move powerfully among us. Tears fell freely, hands were raised in surrender, and the atmosphere shifted from one of hesitation to one of expectation. I saw people letting go of their burdens, their fears, and their distractions, and opening their hearts to the Holy Spirit.

The net wasn't just a metaphor anymore—it became a reality in the lives of those who chose to cast it that day.

I spoke about the importance of surrender. "You cannot hold onto your doubts, your fears, and your distractions and expect to receive all that God has for you," I said. "Surrender them. Lay them down at His feet. The act of casting your net is an act of trust, a declaration that you believe in His power to provide." I reminded them that surrender is not a sign of weakness but of strength. It is the key to experiencing true spiritual transformation.

Throughout the message, I returned to the promise of John 14:26: "The Advocate, the Holy Spirit, whom the Father will send in my name, will teach you all things and will remind you of everything I have said to you." The Holy Spirit is our guide, our teacher, and our helper. But we must be ready to listen, to learn, and to follow His lead. Casting the net is not something we do alone—it is something we do in partnership with Him.

I told the congregation, "The Lord is saying to you today: 'Prepare your nets. Make them larger. Cast them farther.'" But I also reminded them that a larger net comes with greater responsibility. It requires not only faith but also readiness. Are you ready to hold what God is preparing to pour out into your life? Are you prepared to carry the blessings, the opportunities, and the responsibilities that come with them?

I urged them to examine their lives. "What is holding you back from casting your net? Is it fear of failure? Is it the weight of past disappointments? Is it the distractions of this world?" I encouraged them to identify these barriers and to surrender them to God. "Do not let the enemy keep you from stepping into the abundance God has for you," I said. "You have been given the tools, the strength, and the guidance of the Holy Spirit. Use them."

The sermon concluded with a powerful call to action. I invited the congregation to come forward, to stand in faith, and to declare their readiness to cast their nets. As they did, I prayed over them, asking the Holy Spirit to fill them with courage, with faith, and with the assurance of God's promises. The room was filled with the sound of prayers, of worship, and of the Spirit moving among His people.

I reminded them one final time: "The size of your net determines the size of your blessings.
Do not be afraid to cast it wide. Do not be afraid to trust in the God who loves you, who provides for you, and who is always faithful to His word. Be ready to receive what He has for you. And when He fills your net, do not forget to give Him the glory."

That day, I saw a congregation transformed. I saw faith renewed, hearts healed, and lives changed. And I left that place with the deep assurance that God had done something extraordinary among His people. It wasn't my words that made the difference—it was His Spirit, His power, and His promise. To Him be the glory forever.

Biblical Quote: John 14:26, "Be ready to receive it"

As I reflect on the profound words of Jesus in John 14:26, "But the Advocate, the Holy Spirit, whom the Father will send in my name, will teach you all things and will remind you of everything I have said to you," I am reminded of the incredible promise embedded in this verse. It is not merely a statement; it is an assurance, a call, and a divine invitation to experience the Holy Spirit's guiding, comforting, and empowering presence in our lives. These words resonate deeply with me because they form the foundation of faith and trust in God's provision.

When I stood before the congregation to preach this message, the atmosphere was heavy with expectation. I could sense the hunger in their hearts—a yearning for something greater, for the presence of the Holy Spirit to break through the barriers of doubt, fear, and uncertainty. It was clear to me that this was not just another sermon but a divine appointment, a moment for each person to grasp the fullness of God's promise and to be ready to receive it.

I began by drawing attention to the recurring metaphor of the net, a central theme in my message. The net symbolizes our faith—the capacity we have to hold and embrace God's blessings. I told the congregation, "Faith is the net you cast into the unknown, trusting that God will fill it with what you need. The size of your net reflects the size of your trust. If your faith is small, your net will be small, and so will the blessings you can hold.

But if you dare to believe, if you stretch your faith, you will find that God's provision is far greater than you can imagine."

As I spoke these words, I could see the eyes of the congregation light up. They began to grasp the truth of what I was saying—that faith is not passive; it is active. Faith requires action, a willingness to step out even when the outcome is uncertain. It means casting your net into the deep waters of life, believing that God's unseen hand is at work even when you cannot see it.

I shared with them a personal story from my own journey, a time when I felt God calling me to cast my net in faith. It was a season of uncertainty, a moment when I had no guarantee of success, only the assurance that God was leading me. I told them how I wrestled with doubt, questioning whether I had the strength to obey.

But then I remembered the promise of John 14:26—that the Holy Spirit would teach me all things and remind me of Jesus' words. I surrendered my fears and took that leap of faith, and in doing so, I experienced God's provision in ways that exceeded my expectations.

This is what I wanted the congregation to understand: the Holy Spirit is not a distant entity but an ever-present guide, comforter, and source of wisdom. When Jesus promised to send the Advocate, He was giving us the assurance that we would never be alone. The Holy Spirit walks with us, teaches us, and empowers us to face life's uncertainties with confidence.

But to experience this, we must be ready to receive it. We must open our hearts and minds to His leading and trust that His plan is greater than ours.

As I continued to preach, I emphasized the importance of receptivity. "Are you ready to receive it?" I asked them. "Are you prepared to let go of your doubts, your fears, and your distractions so that you can fully embrace what God has for you?" I reminded them that being ready to receive is not just about waiting; it is about preparing. It is about enlarging your net, stretching your faith, and positioning yourself to catch the blessings that God is ready to pour out.

The emotional and spiritual responses in the room were tangible. I could see tears streaming down faces as people wrestled with their own barriers to faith.

There were moments of trembling prayer, heartfelt cries for deliverance, and bursts of joy as the Holy Spirit moved among us. It was a testament to the power of God to transform lives in an instant. I reminded them that these moments were not just emotional experiences but evidence of the Holy Spirit's active work within them.

I also spoke about the connection between faith and action. "Believing without seeing is not easy," I said, "but it is the essence of faith. When you cast your net, you may not see what lies beneath the surface, but you trust that God is there, filling it with His provision."

I urged them to take steps of faith, even when the path ahead seemed unclear. "Faith is not about knowing; it is about trusting," I told them. "It is about taking that first step, believing that God will meet you where you are and lead you to where you need to be."

As the message unfolded, I returned to the metaphor of the net. "The larger your net, the greater the blessings," I said. "But a larger net also requires greater faith. It requires you to stretch beyond your comfort zone, to let go of your limitations, and to trust in God's unlimited power." I encouraged them to ask themselves, "How large is my net? Am I limiting God's blessings because of my fear or doubt? Am I willing to cast my net wider, to trust Him more deeply?"

The sermon concluded with a call to action. I invited the congregation to stand, to lift their hands in surrender, and to declare their readiness to receive.
As they did, I prayed over them, asking the Holy Spirit to fill them with faith, courage, and the assurance of God's promises. The atmosphere was electric with the presence of God, a sacred moment where heaven touched earth and lives were forever changed.

In John 14:26, Jesus promises that the Holy Spirit will teach us all things and remind us of His words. This promise is not just for the disciples of old; it is for each one of us today. The Holy Spirit is our Advocate, our guide, and our source of wisdom. But to experience His power, we must be ready to receive it.

We must prepare our hearts, cast our nets of faith, and trust in God's provision.

As I left the pulpit that day, I felt a deep sense of gratitude for the work God had done among us. It was a reminder that His promises are true, His Spirit is active, and His provision is abundant. To Him be all the glory, forever and ever.

Prophetic Message

As I stood before the congregation, the weight of the moment settled on my heart. I knew this was not just another message; it was a divine call, an invitation to each believer present. "Will you be able to carry the net?" I asked, my voice echoing through the room. This question was not meant to intimidate but to inspire—a challenge that carried within it the promise of God's abundant blessings.

It was a moment to awaken hearts, to stir faith, and to ignite a readiness to receive what God had prepared for them.

I could sense that many in the room were struggling with doubt and fear, weighed down by life's challenges. Yet, I reminded them that the God we serve is not a God of insufficiency but a God of abundance. The net I spoke of symbolized the capacity of their faith—their ability to hold the blessings God desired to pour into their lives. But with greater blessings comes a greater responsibility, and that responsibility begins with trust.

"Prepare your hearts," I urged them. "For the weight of His blessings is not light. It requires a faith that is steadfast, a heart that is ready, and hands willing to labour for His Kingdom." The prophetic words flowed not from me but from the Spirit who filled the room, reminding us all that God's blessings are not random; they are intentional, purposeful, and transformative. But to carry the net, one must first be willing to cast it.

I spoke about the spiritual battles we all face, battles that often seek to weaken our faith and steal our joy. "No evil spirit has to come to you," I proclaimed, my voice firm with the authority of His promise. "In Jesus' name, rebuke the forces that come against you. Stand firm, for the Lord is your protector, your shield, and your fortress." These words were not just a proclamation; they were a reminder that the victory has already been won through Christ. As believers, we are called to stand in that victory, to claim it, and to live in the freedom it provides.

Prayer became a central theme of the prophetic message. I likened it to a spiritual net, one that grows stronger when cast collectively. "When you pray together, your faith unites," I said. "And when your faith unites, the net becomes unbreakable." I called the congregation to fervent prayer, not as individuals isolated in their struggles but as a community bound by faith and purpose. "Pray for one another," I encouraged them. "Lift each other up, for when one stumbles, the others will hold them steady."

The room grew quiet as the words settled into their hearts. I could see the resolve building in their eyes, the determination to stand firm in faith and to trust in God's provision. Prayer is not just a conversation with God; it is an act of spiritual warfare, a declaration of trust, and a means of drawing closer to His presence. Through prayer, we cast our spiritual nets, believing that God will fill them with His abundance.

The prophetic message was not just about preparation; it was about transformation. I reminded them that unwavering faith would bring about a renewal of spirit and a growth that could not be measured. "God is preparing larger nets for you," I told them. "But are you ready to carry them? Are you prepared for the transformation that comes with His blessings?" These questions were meant to stir their spirits, to challenge them to rise above their doubts and to step into the fullness of God's plan for their lives.

Transformation does not come without sacrifice, I explained. It requires letting go of old habits, releasing fears, and surrendering fully to God's will. "The net you carry today may seem heavy," I said, "but with each step of faith, your strength will grow. And soon, you will find that the burdens you once carried have become blessings you now hold."

I spoke of divine Favor, the unmerited grace of God that flows into our lives when we walk in obedience and faith. "God's Favor is not something you earn," I reminded them.

"It is a gift, freely given. But to receive it, your heart must be open, your hands must be ready, and your spirit must be willing." The promises of God are not bound by human limitations; they are limitless, eternal, and overflowing.

As the message unfolded, I felt the Holy Spirit moving among us, breaking chains of doubt and fear, and replacing them with faith and hope. I saw tears streaming down faces, hands lifted in surrender, and hearts opening to the transformative power of God's presence. This was not just a sermon; it was a moment of divine encounter, a time when heaven touched earth, and lives were forever changed.

The prophetic message ended with a call to action. "Step out in faith," I urged them. "Do not wait for the perfect moment, for now is the time. Offer what you have, no matter how small, and watch as God multiplies it for His glory." I reminded them that the miracles of God begin with the resources already in our hands.
Just as Jesus fed the multitudes with a few loaves and fishes, He can take our small offerings and turn them into something extraordinary.

"Love must drive your response," I said. "Compassion is the heart of God's mission, and it must be the heart of ours as well." I encouraged them to look beyond themselves, to see the needs of others, and to act in faith and love. "When you unite in purpose," I told them, "you will see the power of God move in ways you never thought possible."

The prophetic message was a reminder that we are not alone in this journey. Together, as a community of faith, we can accomplish far greater works for God's Kingdom than we ever could alone. It is in unity, in shared purpose, and in collective faith that we find the strength to carry the nets God has prepared for us.

As I concluded, I prayed over the congregation, asking God to fill their nets with His blessings, to strengthen their faith, and to prepare their hearts for the journey ahead. "Go forth," I told them, "not in fear but in faith, not in doubt but in trust. For the Lord has called you, and He has equipped you. Be ready to receive it, and watch as His promises unfold in your life."

This was not just a message; it was a movement, a call to rise, to trust, and to carry the nets of faith into a world in need. And as I left the pulpit, I knew that God had begun a new work in the hearts of His people, a work that would bear fruit for His Kingdom.

Reflection and Application

The sermon invited individuals to reflect on their spiritual readiness. How often do we hesitate to cast the net of faith because of fear or uncertainty? This question resonated deeply, encouraging self-examination and a renewed commitment to trust God. The preacher highlighted the necessity of confronting both internal doubts and external challenges with faith. God's power, they reminded the congregation, is sufficient to overcome any obstacle.

The repeated call to "be ready to receive it" served as a reminder to trust in God's timing. The sermon encouraged believers to embrace the waiting period as an essential part of their faith journey. Faith was presented not as a one-time act but as a lifestyle—a continuous casting of the net, a daily readiness to receive God's guidance and blessings. Practical steps for cultivating faith included regular prayer, studying scripture, and remaining open to the Holy Spirit's prompting. The congregation was urged to live with a constant expectation of God's miraculous work in their lives.

The South African sermon of 2016 remains a profound reminder of the power of faith and the readiness required to receive God's blessings. The metaphor of the net challenges believers to expand their capacity for grace, trust, and obedience. As the preacher declared, "The net is already in front of you. Will you cast it?" This question calls us all to action, encouraging a life of unwavering faith and spiritual readiness to embrace the fullness of God's plan.

Soldiers of The Cross Ministry
909 S. 3rd Avenue
Wausau Wisconsin
54403 (715) 212-1575
Reverend Dr. Antony Walto,

Soldiers of the Cross is very honoured to congratulate you on the publishing of your book. We are excited to have been able to be part of the last 10+ years of your ministry. We are thrilled about your future endeavours, and we look forward to many more rich years of your friendship. Soldiers of the Cross wishes you blessings and miracles beyond measure as you take the words God has given you and use them to bless every person.
May your book serve to change the lives of the people who read it. May it serve a positive testimony to the work you have done to become the accomplished Child of God that you are today

.

In Christ,
Bishop Benjamin Paris
Bishop Benjamin Paris
Founder of Soldiers of the cross United
World Wide
www.sotcunited.org
Outreach Pastor with Gilead Church and Ministry
Wausau Wisconsin
https://gileadchurch.online/

Chapter 5 –
6 Oct 2022 India

He was amazed at their lack of faith. Then Jesus went around teaching from the village. "Amazed by Unbelief" Mark 6:6

"Amazed by Unbelief"

Let us trace out what this theme "Amazed by Unbelief" means to us. Imagine Jesus' life: He comes back to His hometown, where the bulk of its people have known Him since childhood, had witnessed His life, but could not believe although He performed miracles and taught. Mark 6:6 captures the moment: *"He was amazed at their lack of faith. Then he went around teaching from village to village."*
Here we see the humanity of Jesus, feeling sad and maybe even disappointed. He knew these people; he knew their faces; yet he saw in them a refusal to believe, a barrier to their very own blessings.

This is a historic and yet very personal moment, one that I face every day in my own life: How often do I doubt, seeing what He does in my own experience? Jesus's words, directed to those around His miracles, become an in-your-face reminder for believers like me: not with unbelievers who did not know Him but with men and women who had actually known Him.

This reaction should challenge us to look at our hearts and see where we might also be holding back in faith. It is easy to believe when everything is going well, but the real test of faith is when doubt creeps in despite all we have seen and experienced.

Faith and unbelief are two opposing forces that Mold our spiritual journey. So essentially the concept of unbelief goes on to become the basic denial, locking the inmost self against the truth and power of God. When Jesus encountered such unbelieving people back in his hometown, he didn't step back from his missionary work but instead progressed onward with his teaching in more cities and towns. And as we learn from that moment's act, we ought not to step back against opponents and doubts in advance. Jesus' ministry was too precious to allow a lack of faith around him to stop him. And so should not our faith walk be stopped by doubt and the unbelief of others. Jesus reminds us that in his case, our own mission to grow in faith, to spread God's love, cannot be stilled.
This scene is also a call to ponder how unbelief can also be a barrier between God's miracles and us. As we have unbelief, God can't work from inside us. Faith opens up the door for God's might and miracles to happen. And just as Jesus was unable to do many miracles in his hometown because of little faith, we will also miss out on God's blessing when we harbour unbelief. It is not as if God's power somehow is lessened; rather, our openness to receiving it is blocked. Faith is like a bridge-it connects us to God's supernatural abilities, allowing His grace to flow into our lives.

Today, as you read this, I encourage you to look within. Ask yourself honestly: Is there an area of my life where unbelief has taken root? Maybe you've been in one of these situations where there seemed like no way forward and not because you handed over such a situation totally to God, but then, questions began popping up in your heart; "Can He intervene on this?" Perhaps, a dream you stopped trying hard for, it was just because unbelief constantly tells you these are unrealistic. Jesus' amazement at unbelief is not only a moment in history; it's a living reminder that faith forms the essence of being immersed in God's presence and power.

Faith acts as the base of a relationship between a human being and God. It can be regarded as the viewfinder of how His hands are visible in one's life. In the lack of it, we lose the blessings that He urgently wants to pour out onto us like those people during Jesus' time in His hometown. Faith is not believing in the existence of God. Faith is believing in His goodness, believing in His timing, believing in His purpose. Faith believes He is working all things out for our good, though we cannot see it now.

I challenge you today: Where does your faith need to be strengthened? Where have walls of unbelief built up in your heart, and you need to have them broken down? It's not a question to hurry through but to really ask yourself. God is asking you to take in something greater, deeper, and more profound about the presence of God, and that involves faith. This requires releasing control, casting away doubt, and then opening the heart fully to Him.

And like Jesus, who continued to teach even though the unbelieving surrounded Him, so we must keep on moving forward, keeping our faith alive and God able to work in His perfect will in our lives.

This call to introspection over unbelief is a call to transformation. It is not about wallowing in guilt or shame for having doubts; it is about recognizing that you can choose faith even if doubts are trying to seep into your heart. Remember, even the disciples, who saw the miracles firsthand, had their moments of doubt. Faith is not a decision but a journey- a daily commitment to trust God more and more. Let this passage, "He was amazed at their lack of faith," ring in your heart as a reminder that God's desire for us is unwavering trust. He wants to reveal His power, to work miracles, to bless us abundantly. But we need to open the door of our hearts fully and let our faith welcome His presence into every corner of our lives. Today, make this your prayer: *"Lord, help me overcome my unbelief. Strengthen my faith, that I may receive all that You have prepared for me."* May I not be among those who knew you but doubted, but rather to be counted with the others who believe without pause, who trust You completely. Let me walk with You in faith; let me find myself amazed, not at the depth of my lack of faith, but at what God does in and among us.

Sermon Preached by the Prophet

Let us take this to heart and allow it to reshape how we live our faith each day. As He walked among those who doubted Him, Jesus did not rebuke them in anger but used the moment to speak profoundly about the nature of true faith. He didn't let their lack of faith stop Him from continuing with His mission. He would go on teaching and doing miracles despite the opposition. His work would press on no matter what opposition came it's way, and so we learn from this: that our faith journey is not only overcoming doubts but also persevering in action and trust even when doubts threaten to cloud one's vision.

The Prophet goes one step further by reminding us that faith is a living force that compels us to do God's will. Faith is not just mere passive belief; it demands action. As James 2:26 puts it, "Faith without works is dead." Faith is, therefore, a commitment to trust both in beliefs and actions.

It shows the world that we believe in His promises and trust in His power, for He is as powerful and present in our lives today as He was in the days of the disciples. This kind of faith is what will become the basis of our life as it reflects God's love, grace, and purpose.

In his sermon, the Prophet shared several testimonies of how he witnessed miracles—stories of healing, provision, and transformation that underscore the truth of God's active presence.

These testimonies are more than inspiring tales; they are concrete reminders that God is working here and now. But these miracles are not only in the stories we hear; they are invitations, calling us to believe that what God has done in others' lives, He can also do in ours. The Reverend's words reminded us that faith is the key to opening the door to these miracles. Our faith is not about merely acknowledging God's existence but about trusting in His power to intervene and transform our situations.

Just think of being among the disciples, watching the miracles of Jesus day after day. It would seem that daily exposure to such displays of divine power would leave no room for doubt. Even the disciples, who walked closest to Him, had their moments of unbelief. It is something of the human element we can all relate to. We, too, have seasons of uncertainty when our faith is wavering. The Reverend here made the message on an even deeper level to tell us how we need to remove those doubts by standing firm and grounded in God's word.

Our faith ought to be built upon His promises and the veracity of His Word to give us the energy not to let doubt conquer or get the better of our minds.

The Prophet urged us to confront and challenge any lingering unbelief that may be hindering us from experiencing God's full blessing. This requires a conscious effort to examine our hearts, acknowledge where doubt may have crept in, and actively choose faith over fear. Let us not be passive in our faith but bold and proactive, seeking to deepen our trust in God.

As the Reverend pointed out we need to be on guard for methods by which the unbelief must be brought out; our faith, after all, is the very key through which the power of God works into and through us.

In these moments, we're reminded that faith is a gift, yet it is also a choice. We can place our trust in God every day, and He will lead us to believe that He is faithful to fulfil His promises. Let us be disciples walking in active faith, prepared to witness the miracles prepared for us. It challenges the reader to move above doubt, into the fullness of God's blessings and therefore encourages us to live out our faith with an unwavering commitment to God, even in the face of such challenges.

Biblical Quote: Mark 6:6 - "He was amazed at their lack of faith. Then Jesus went around teaching from village to village."

This verse speaks to us on so many levels. Imagine the heart of Jesus, who had come with love, power, and a mission to bring healing and salvation to all, only to be met with scepticism by those closest to Him. These were the people who probably saw Him grow up; perhaps they had heard the whispers of His wisdom, and seen hints of His divinity. Yet, before the fullness of who He was, they could not bring themselves to believe. This amazement of Jesus at their unbelief is both a reminder and a warning for us. If those who stood in His presence could doubt Him, we, too, can fall into the trap of unbelief when we allow our familiarity with the concept of Jesus to cloud our faith.

We get so used to hearing about God's power and promises in our lives that they become ordinary things we hear. We hear about miracles, but do we believe that they could happen for us? We read about His love, but do we let that love change us daily? Jesus was surprised not so much by their disbelief but by the reflection of an unresponsive heart—a heart that saw and could not recognize, a heart that heard and could not understand. This reaction by Jesus stirs something inside us. We are led to ask if we have grown so comfortable with Jesus that we do not marvel anymore at him. Faith is the door through which God enters our lives with His blessings, grace, and miracles.

Without faith, we can become spiritually stagnant, closed off from the vibrant, living relationship God wants to share with us. Jesus saw how their unbelief prevented them from receiving the fullness of what He had to offer, and it saddened Him. He didn't need their faith to be validated; His mission and identity were secure. But He knew that their faith—or lack thereof—was critical to them living the life of the Kingdom.

We can learn that our faith is not what we think but rather something about openness to the transformation God is allowing to occur in us. The verse speaks also to perseverance. Jesus did not tarry in disappointment because of the lack of faith in His hometown. Instead, He proceeded to preach from town to town. Here is what we learn from it: even when facing opposition or doubt, we are not to tarry or retreat. The call to proclaim God's love and His truth continues, irrespective of how that message is received.

To each of us, it is the encouragement of Jesus, as he faces disbelief at his hands, whether by men or in our hearts: in all that God has set before us to do, we need to lean into our faith and push forward. In a world where scepticism usually reigns and faith is shaken, we often get discouraged when people do not receive God's love as we want them to. However, like Jesus, we will have to keep on persevering and continue spreading God's message of love for the simple reason that "God's power is best displayed in weakness."

His love, truth, and grace, therefore continue to be given to all the willing recipients. This passage also underscores so strongly an important part of faith: it is not passive; it is to start acting with God, to trust Him enough to allow that to shape us into, our actions, our responses, and our perspective. Faith is living so your life demonstrates trust in what God has promised, does, and is with us, even when the folks around you doubt.

As we are encouraged to do this just as Jesus went through villages and towns where some doubted Him, so will we be called upon, with boldness, to continue serving, loving, and proclaiming His truth - even when things seem unworkable. On reflection on this scripture, I should also think about ways faithlessness could even become an unnoticed thing in our lives. Perhaps a lingering doubt about God heals and mends broken relationships, or possibly I do not believe God can provide for all needs, or perhaps I do not feel that He can utilize me in really meaningful ways.

These small seeds of unbelief, if not nipped in the bud, may prevent us from really enjoying the full depth of God's power and presence.

Jesus was disappointed that people didn't believe because He knew that their lack of faith would keep them from receiving what He was so ready to give. This reminds us to step out of our comfort zone. To properly receive what God has for us, we must let go of our restrictions on Him, for His ways are higher than ours and His powers are beyond our comprehension. Jesus' hometown folk missed out on the experience of His miracles because they could not see past their preconceptions about who they thought He was. And we might miss the miraculous if we limit our faith to what we can understand.

This verse calls for a living, breathing faith, not one of mere acknowledgment but one that expects God's intervention. We are called to look at the area of doubt in ourselves and seek a new perspective by being open to the full scope of what God can do. In coming to Him with faith, we open ourselves to a transforming, powerful, and very personal relationship. Let's be careful then and avoid familiarity or doubt clouding our faith. Let our hearts be renewed constantly, as we ask God to revive our faith, so we can receive everything He intends for us. Even as Jesus continued His ministry with those who doubted around Him, we too have to carry on in our lives based on trust in God's plan for our lives.

And as we journey, keep us mindful of a faith that is bright, firm, and can take us through all life's seasons.

And the question falls to each one of us: Will we be, like those who knew him in Jesus' own hometown- dulled by familiarity- or will we come unto God with open hearts and ready belief and ready arms to receive His miracles within our lives? That is the challenge set before us- to run towards a living, hope-filled faith based on God's unchanging love and power. May we not meet that challenge but become that light of faith that changes not only our lives but touches the lives of those around us, drawing them into the wonder and majesty of a life lived with true belief.

Prophetic Message

Today, I feel the urge to share with you a prophetic message that calls us to an urgent examination of our faith. Faith is no convenience but rather the very foundation of our relationship with God. It is what binds us to His promises, to His power, and His very presence in our lives. Without faith, we drift. We go about, unable to get our bearings, and miss that full, life-changing life God has set before us. This is a call, a call to our faith, and to keep it alive and active in our daily walk with the Lord. This message is not subtle-it's urgent. While God is infinitely patient, desiring that none should be lost, He also warns us not to test His patience with complacency. *"Do not test the Lord your God,"* we are reminded. This isn't a threat but a call to awaken, to shake off the sluggishness of spiritual neglect, and to respond with urgency and commitment. Faith isn't something to defer; it's our lifeline to God's will and purpose.

He is calling His people into revival, a revival that is found in each of our individual choices to trust all the way, commit all the way, and believe all the way. This is the time to act by drawing near to Him without reluctance, embracing life in all its fullness.

God's Spirit is moving in ways that are deep and powerful, looking to pour out blessings, wisdom, and renewal on those who are ready. Those who open their hearts in full belief will find themselves strengthened in ways they could never have imagined. They will receive guidance, peace, and the courage to face the unknown knowing that God goes before them.
The Holy Spirit is looking for vessels to fill, hearts to transform, and lives ready to shine His light to a world that is desirous of hope. This call is not made for our sake but rather for the sake of the people around us who are so desperately in need of God's love, mercy, and truth.

Thc prophetic word today again comes with the promise that healing and miracles are to happen to all believers. While Jesus would always perform a miracle to someone who was approaching him with faith, God also does it the same way even today for those among whom He remains yesterday, today, and forever. All promises are not for the select few but for all willing to believe. But faith is not passive; faith demands us to step out and take a leap in the dark, letting go of our fears and doubts and embracing the unknown in total confidence in God's promise. Miracles happen when faith sets fire; healing flows when belief opens doors.

However, there is a divine guidance associated with this prophetic utterance: do not have doubts to delay following God. Like Jesus, we, too, are challenged to walk in faith even as it appears to face disbelief and rejection in the future. Tenacity is required for faith; it calls one forward while trusting that God is doing His thing, no matter how things look when one cannot see what they look like. It means that walking in faith is moving on, step by step when the way is not obvious. It's the confident expectation that God will shed light upon the path we take as we proceed and give us just what we need at the very moment required.

We are entering into a season of revival, a season to rekindle our hearts renew our minds, and breathe new life into our spirits. This revival is not something that we wait for passively but something we engage actively in. It is a time when we fan the flames of our faith, recommit ourselves to God's will, and welcome the work of the Holy Spirit with open arms. The prophetic message of the day today is a call to prepare oneself, be watchful in one's faith, and wait for God's blessings to flow because His purposes will align themselves within us.

This revival begins within each one of us individually and collectively. It is a call to shed the doubts tear down the walls of unbelief and open oneself completely to God's transforming power. May our hearts become fertile ground for seeds of faith to grow and yield lives reflective of His love, His mercy, and His glory before the world.

Let us rise to this opportunity by giving ourselves to the seriousness of this prophetic message, to a new season of faith, and to understanding that God is with us, that he will guide us through it all, making us ready to carry this light. We have to be willing to respond to this call because God, who calls, will certainly come to fulfil all that He said He would do.

Lessons for Believers

As we close this chapter, I want to leave you with practical lessons for living a life of unwavering faith. These principles are not just ideas; they are meant to be implemented, guiding us as we deepen our walk with God.
Let them serve as a roadmap for strengthening our faith, overcoming areas of unbelief, and becoming a testimony of God's power in the world.

Understanding the Role of Doubt: Doubt, though challenging, is a natural part of our spiritual journey. It's not something we should ignore or feel ashamed of. Instead, we can view doubt as an invitation to bring our concerns before God. When we openly bring our doubts to Him in prayer, He can use those moments to build a stronger, more resilient faith. Take a moment to reflect on any lingering doubts you may have about God's promises, His love, or His ability to work in your life. Approach Him honestly and allow His Spirit to guide you through them. Remember, even the disciples wrestled with doubt despite witnessing miracles firsthand.

Prayer, studying the Word, and surrounding ourselves with faithful believers can transform our doubts into opportunities for growth.

Faith as a Daily Practice: Faith is not a one-time decision; it's a commitment we renew each day. Every morning, we face the choice to trust in God's promises, to lean into His wisdom, and to invite His presence into our lives. By intentionally dedicating time each day to prayer and reflection, we set the tone for a life rooted in faith. This daily practice strengthens our relationship with God and equips us to face the uncertainties and challenges of life with a steadfast heart. Just as we nurture our physical health daily, so must we feed our faith, keeping it vibrant and alive. Consider setting aside time each day for prayer, gratitude, or reading the Word.

The more we build this habit, the stronger our faith becomes, and the more we can witness God's transforming power in our lives.

Recognizing God's Power: God is continuously at work around us, in ways both big and small. Often, it's easy to overlook the blessings He has woven into our lives, especially in the routine or challenging moments. But when we begin to view life through a lens of gratitude, we become more attuned to His power at work. Every answered prayer, every peaceful moment, every connection with others—all of these are evidence of His presence. Cultivate a heart that sees God's hand in your life, even in the simplest blessings.

A life of faith includes keeping our eyes open for the beauty of His creation, the provision of our daily needs, and the moments of comfort He provides in times of hardship. Let gratitude become the fuel that feeds your faith, drawing you closer to Him as you recognize His constant care and power.

Responding to God's Word: The Bible tells us, "Faith without works is dead." True faith compels us to action—it isn't passive but rather dynamic, influencing how we live, love, and serve. When we read the Word and hear His teachings, we are called to live them out. This is what distinguishes belief from faith; belief acknowledges, but faith acts. Let God's teachings inspire you to reach out, serve, and love others. Faith that is lived out becomes a powerful testimony to those around us. It might be in small ways—helping a neighbour, being patient with someone in need, offering words of encouragement.

Each act rooted in faith is an extension of God's love and a step in growing His kingdom. As we respond to His Word, let our actions reflect our commitment to Christ, demonstrating a love that mirrors His.

Encouragement for Spiritual Growth: Finally, commit yourself to ongoing spiritual growth. A relationship with God is like any other; it requires time, attention, and intentionality. Seek out fellowship with other believers, as the encouragement and support of a faith community are essential in this journey. Attend gatherings, study groups, or prayer meetings where you can draw strength from others' experiences and insights.

These connections can uplift us, inspire us, and provide wisdom when we face our challenges. Surround yourself with believers who encourage your faith, who remind you of God's goodness, and who walk alongside you as you grow in Him. Regularly engage with God's Word, allow the Spirit to guide you, and ask God to deepen your understanding. The more we invest in our relationship with Him, the closer we will draw to His heart, and the more we will see His presence in every aspect of our lives. The journey of faith is one of continual transformation. This chapter, "Amazed by Unbelief," is a challenge to rise above doubt, to trust fully, and to live with a heart surrendered to God. Let us respond to this call with open hearts, willing to trust, ready to act, and committed to growing closer to Him every day. May we be a people of unwavering faith, a light in a world in need, and a living testimony of God's power and love? As we step forward, may we do so with confidence, assured that God walks with us and that He will complete the work He has begun in each of us.

CANADA 150
TORONTO

Big congratulation Rev. Dr. Antony Walto on your publication of your new book. The book is really inspiring and a blessing to many souls. I appreciate the impact you are making in the body of Christ in your Evangelistic, crusade and mobilization outreach all over the world. Our God will bless you immensely.

This is to let you know that we in Greater Glory Global Kings palace mission Int'L. Nigeria West Africa. Are so blessed with the book. Many are testifying of its great impacts in their Christian lives / Journey. Much more grace my fellow labourer in God's vane yard.
I pray that God will divinely secure you, bless you the more, use you the more and keep you till His day. Much more Grace.

Rupturable. Shalom
APST. DR. PRINCE JERRY O.
TEL: 08033177083 Address: Behind Community Transformer Umuawuchi,
Ihitte-Uboma LGA Imo State.
EMAIL: 3gkpmhq@gmail.com

Chapter 6 –
27th April 2014
Liverpool, Australia.

"Do Not Love the World or the Things in the World" (1 John 2:15)

The Sermon Preached by the Prophet

As I stood before the congregation this day, a deep sense of urgency stirred inside me, a calling resonating deeply in the spirit. Today's word is more than a reminder; it's a call—a call for each of us to know, listen, and respond to the divine plan that God has so carefully placed within us. It is not a gentle invitation to consider but a command urging us to rise, leave behind the comforts that hold us back, and embrace the path that God has set. Every believer has a purpose, a unique role in God's Kingdom, but it takes courage and faith to say, "Here I am, Lord," and to step forward into that purpose. Often, we feel that gentle nudge by the Holy Spirit, that soft whisper of "there is more to come." How many times again do we feel insufficient, as though we are not good enough, not worthy enough? And that is a lie, my friends. God is called us not in terms of qualifications or strengths; His call is founded in His power, purpose, and plan, not ours. Our job isn't to understand but obey.

In this message, I also spoke of one of the most challenging aspects of living out our faith—detachment from the things of this world. Scripture is very clear about this: "Do not love the world nor the things in the world." But how do we understand this in practical terms? This command means that our hearts cannot be divided. We cannot cling to both the eternal and the temporary. To walk fully in God's path requires readiness to let go of attachments, be it material possessions or status, or even relationships that adjust the focus away from Him. Only with the release of these vices can we take a step into God's purpose. Faith as the foundation upon which our relation with God is built keeps us steady, particularly during the tests that we face in life. Faith gives the strength to look beyond the present circumstances and trust the promises of God. I speak from my life-remembering the times I felt lost, the times that the road seemed impossible. But when I had surrendered to these moments, it was then that God's strength became evident, guiding me through. It was in such black hours that miracles occurred by holding onto Him. God's power is manifested as such when we put all our burdens within His hands.

Real faith, however is not a feeling or attitude. It's an active response, living obedience to God's word. Faith which does not manifest itself in action is no faith at all. The Bible is full of people whose obedience led into blessing. Imagine Abraham, who set out from familiar ground-not because he wholly understood but because he trusted God's call to lead him into the unknown.

It is a kind of faith that God asks of us-a faith that moves even when the destination is still unclear. Obedience is somehow always rewarded in God's Kingdom.

And so, as the message drew to a close, I invited people to take a step of faith and step forward: Trust that His hand is upon you, and that His plan, though unseen in the present, would unfold into time. And blessings come in those things we least expect, only for those who take a step of faith. And we, as believers, are called to a life of trust, not comfort. And when we put our trust totally in Him, God can work in us the most profound things.

The scripture in today's reading sets the heart of this message. It is an appeal not to love this world nor the things within it (1 John 2:15). A world of distractions has made it hard for people to focus on what truly matters. God's word is plain on this: 'Do not love the world nor the things in it.' The meaning is simple, but very profound; our hearts must be more for heavenly treasure than earthly treasure. Material wealth and success, even the kind of achievements that some would want to cherish, become the worst idols when placed before God. Indeed, in His presence alone are true joy and satisfaction found-not in accumulation, but in communion with Him. God's love is not this kind, but unconditional and eternal, unlike this love of the world, conditionally dispensed and for only a moment. The world's love is fickle and kept back by the mercy of circumstances. He, however, is love that stands and endures for eternity. And when we turn the heart from the world to God, we find that this Love fills every vacuum: a love that will never leave.

There are numerous distractions in the modern world that, left unchecked, can carry us away from God: technology, and the pursuit of status. I implored the assembly to guard their hearts and be vigilant since our relationship with God needs to take precedence. And Jesus Himself resisted worldly temptations in order to demonstrate that it is indeed possible to live in this world but not be a part of it. Since scripture warns us about the grip of worldly attachment, God promises to provide all our needs. We have to trust Him to seek His Kingdom first; He shall be faithful to fulfil all our needs. The following is the assurance: God's care toward us does not waver, and His provisions lack nothing. With our burden upon the earth laid to one side and our hope in Him, we open ourselves fully unto His blessings

"Do Not Love the World or the Things in the World" – A Call to Faithful Focus

Let's dip into what we might find in 1 John 2:15. Do not love the world or the things in the world. This is not just a word of caution against something, but it is, in fact, a call to realign our lives. It's actually challenging us to move out of the lenses that capture our earthly distractions and centre in on a relationship with God. In this context, the apostle explains how love for the world and its temporary pleasures can take us far from the divine path as well as bring nonfulfillment because only God's eternal love will bring fulfilment. Therefore, the call to be detached from the world is not a call to reject life's blessings but to understand where our true security as well as fulfilment lies.

Separation unto the things of the world is essential to bring a heart full of God. This easily overshadows God and can lead one to place his trust in what he sees and touches, forgetting about the reality of God's unseen presence. The world gives one wealth and status, but both the rewards are only temporary. To the apostle, worldly riches are nothing as compared to God's love and grace. We, by giving preference to God instead of earthly riches, are now open to peace, joy, and satisfaction that would result from our lives being anchored in His presence.

The apostle develops this further by giving us the biblical take on love. Worldly love, on the other hand, is almost of a conditional nature. It goes through different conditions, emotions, and even personal gain.

However, God's love is quite the opposite of that kind-eternal, unconditional, and not fleeting. He loves us regardless of our achievements or our possessions. The brief nature of worldly love is in total contrast to the firmness of God's love. The apostle underlines that our seeking of love and acceptance must be seen for God, whose love fills every vacuum and remains faithful when all else fails. However, this knowledge would not help us till we learn to understand that only His love can bring fulfilment and therefore focus attention on building a relationship with God.

This appeal in our modern time is pretty challenging for one to disentangle one from the love of the world because we live in a world where technology, social media, and status determine our actions-and as for our sense of worth. The apostle shows that the temptations exemplified within the book at that moment are also being experienced at the moment. Just as early believers were held captive by the social attractions bestowed upon them, modern believers must curb attachments to technology, money, and recognition. The extent to which we orient our lives around these things, the true priority that goes on our lives, is actually usurping the relationship with God in ways that we seek satisfaction in something fleeting. The apostle turns his readers' attention to the fact that they live in this world and are not to centre their attention on the temporal; instead, they should remain acutely alert to the vision of God's plan for us.

This is certainly not a message of control or denial. While warning us not to love the world, the apostle also comforts God's faithful provision. He says that putting God first in place of worldly concerns is not left in want. God will provide to His children according to His wisdom and grace. Of course, the apostle reminds the congregation that God's provision is not necessarily according to our mundane desires but ever sufficient, ever on time, and always in our best interest. Such assurance allows Christians to drop their fears and anxieties that often accompany materialistic things. Trusting in God's provision allows us to be at peace in the love of God, knowing He knows and meets every aspect of our need.
The call of the apostle is into things that really matter, for one to focus attention on a relationship with God than anything else, and one will realize that the highest reward for life is in His love and presence. It has enabled us to contemplate being delivered from running after temporary pleasures; we are called into following a life of faith, with contentment, gratitude, and trust in God's perfect plan.

Let's look into our own hearts as we consider this teaching. Where are we finding our trust, our self-worth? What is holding us back in life from fully embracing God's love? This verse in 1 John serves as a gentle reminder to let go of something or someone holding us back from a life of pure faith and devotion. We choose to love God more than this world at every decision, every act of worship, every surrender. But then we find that it is only in this choice that we discover depth, peace, and strength within a life lived close to the heart of God.

May this message inspire us to refocus, putting God in the centre of our lives and walking in the assurance of His eternal love and provision. We shall enjoy our journey into the future, not seeking what the world can give but rejoicing in the incomparable and everlasting love of our Creator.

The Prophetic Message

Today I have the urgency to share a prophetic message that carries deep in its heart a call to action, urging each of us to act in faith without hesitation. The Holy Spirit is moving upon our lives, stirring in our hearts the call to an immediate response, without procrastination. There is a divine urgency in the air, an unmistakable pull to answer God's voice with an unwavering "yes." This is a call to rise, to shake off any doubt, and to move forward in trust and boldness. God is not looking for those who wait or hesitate but for those who will step out in faith, ready to embrace the purpose He has placed within them.

This call to action is clear: God, from His perspective, asks each of us to take the step forward in our journey with Him. Now He invites us to let go of fear, overcome the distractions and doubts that the enemy tries to place in our path, and act boldly. The enemy wants us to wait; he wants us to doubt. But today, I want to tell you something: God's power is larger than whatever is limiting you. For a determined heart that steps forward, even if the way ahead is obscure, unlocks the doors to blessings we cannot imagine. The promises of God are that which lie on the other side of our "yes." He moves when he has answered to his call in ways beyond human understanding.

I shared with you all in this message a dream God is leading His people to a place of abundance. It is not less the material benedictions; rather, it speaks of the word spiritual satisfaction, purpose, peace, and joy, where God alone can give such things. Imagine God leading you down a path where His presence is all around, peace overflows, and joy is constantly present. That's the promise for those in whom we have placed our trust and follow. God has prepared places of blessing, growth, and fulfilment in His plan for each one of us. However, we must move forward with faith to reach those places. Those who will choose to trust will find themselves in places they could never have dreamed of—places cultivated by God Himself.

There are limitless blessings awaiting us, especially for those walking in obedience. There is a certain joy and strength in saying yes to God's call-the fullness that touches every part of our lives. In responding with open hearts and willing spirits, God meets us in the place of obedience with provision and grace. The Holy Spirit already is working, clearing away the obstacles in the path ahead and removing barriers for those prepared to step out in faith. God is not waiting for perfect people; He is waiting for willing hearts. Our blessings multiply when we take Him at His word and act on it, for God honours faith that moves.

But with those promises comes a different warning: don't delay obedience because of your hesitation. I warn you today: not to hasten obedience may mean missing the divine opportunities God has put in our path.

When He calls, His timing is perfect, and so needs your response. There's grace and Favor in His speaking unto us, but if we don't respond quickly, the window of opportunity may close. God is calling His people to be ready, to be alert, and to be active in their faith. This is not the time to dawdle over a decision; this is a time to be decisive and bold.

The message did conclude by reminding of the times: We are living through a season of rapid change, and God is powerful work; He's inviting each of us to be a part of it. Now is the time, and we can't miss the opportunity to respond. Let us step out in faith. The more we do that, the more God will meet us at those places. He will provide, strengthen, and equip us to fulfil our purpose in His Kingdom

Lessons for the Congregation

As we close today's message let's remember some very practical lessons for carrying forward in our walk of faith. They are more than concepts-they are principles, and foundations to build a life on-a life built on trust, service, and commitment to God's purpose. Provided we remember and accept these lessons, it becomes possible to live a life reflecting God's love, grace, and faithfulness in a way that would not only mark our life but also others' lives in the present time as well as the lives of those who come later.

The first one is to trust in God's will and not our wishes. We often have dreams and ambitions and plans to which we hold tight, but the real growth in faith takes this degree of surrender. It calls to rid ourselves of our very own goals for trusting that God's plan is not only the better one but also the fulfilling one, even though it doesn't align with our ambitions. There's a depth of peace and joy when we recognize that we are putting our desires in the hands of God who can see all things, and He sees the full picture. The apostle said, "Giving up something does not necessarily mean that we are giving up"; it simply means that we must give room to God's proper time. It is in these moments of surrender that we experience the fullness of His wisdom and love, realizing that His way is infinitely higher than ours.

Another important lesson learned is that faith without action is hollow. Belief is foundational, but incomplete, if it does not lead to action. Faith is a dynamic force-a force that should propel us forward. To act in faith is a reflection of our trust in God and commitment to His work. The apostle reminded us that true faith is much more than just agreeing with God's promises-it involves stepping out, taking risks, and making choices representative of our beliefs. Faith compels us to serve, love, and go out for others. And so, while we reach to line our lives with our faith, God can use us as a vessel to pour into the lives of people and community; all this, in ways beyond our ultimate understanding.

To serve is the very core of God's calling for each one of us. Service is not limited to ministry alone; it could be as simple as an act of kindness, a word of encouragement, or helping someone in need. Every small act of service counted to God. The apostle encouraged us to look for opportunities to serve others daily. When we live with hearts of service, then we align ourselves with God's purpose, which is marked by the compassion and love of Jesus. Living with such a heart brings us the joy of giving, fulfilment of purpose, and connection to others that strengthens our community of faith.

Doubt overcome by prayer is another great lesson. Doubts are quite an automatic part of the human life, and often, these doubts obscure our faith to the extent that we question the God's promises. However, the apostle requested us to consider prayer as our greatest tool against doubt. When we bring our uncertainties before God in prayer, we ask for His strength to live with us. Prayer is a channel through which we receive guidance, assurance, and peace. It reminds us that we are not walking alone and that God is ever-present, ready to hold our hands when we stumble.

He builds resilience in us through prayer as our trust is strengthened, giving us the courage to face all the battles of the world with confidence and peace.

And so, finally, he talks about the legacy we build. Every choice we make, every step of faith we take, and every act of love we offer contributes to a legacy that can affect generations.

Living a life of obedience and trust creates a foundational faith legacy that transcends our individual lives. It will influence our children and grandchildren; then, by God's grace, others will also be influenced. This legacy of faith has endured far beyond the material goods and achievements. It is a beacon of hope and an example of unshakability and proof of God's faithfulness. That is why we, individuals, should try to leave a legacy that perhaps only fully represents God's love and truth, a foundation that can really be stepped on in confidence.

Let us go on with these lessons in our hearts. God has a purpose for us - one that is both profound and personal. Whether today or tomorrow, there is always the chance to get closer to God, to serve with love, to trust beyond what we can see, and to pray with earnestness. Let these lessons guide us, strengthen us, and encourage us to live lives honouring God and impacting those around us. May we walk in faith, following God's call, and leaving for others a legacy of undying devotion to Him.

May we take these words to heart, responding to God's call with a "yes" that is steadfast and unwavering. Let us live a life that not only believes but acts, a life that reflects God's love, grace, and purpose. As we step forward, may we do so with confidence, knowing that God is with us every step of the way.

November 4, 2024
Rev. Dr. Antony Walto!
Praise the Lord! Congratulations on the publication of your book. We here at Faith Ministries Church are blessed to know you and have been recipients of your anointed ministry here in Columbus, OH USA.
We know that you will reach, touch, and change many people through this book. God bless you on your continued and growing global outreach!
Yours in Christ,
Mr. C. Hype
Dr. C. Dexter Wise III
Pastor Faith Ministries Church
www.FaithMinistries.Church
International President and founder of IFFM
www.IFFMUS.net

Chapter 7 –

22nd April 2013
Time out Mission International World Conference London, UK

"Let's Go to the Other Side of the Lake," (Luke 8:22)

Faith's Journey: Stepping Into the Boat and Trusting God's Plan

Imagine standing on the shore of a vast lake, presented with a decision: stay in your spot where you are safe but stagnant, or step onto a boat promising to carry you over to the other side. No, it is not the passage across the water; it is the journey of faith, the journey toward the purpose God places on your life. And here we are, each of us deciding whether to hold on to what we know or trust in all and in all God's calling on our lives. Today, I feel led by God to guide us through this walk. I have chosen the boat as a metaphoric tool for this walk that He and I have done with Him.

The boat is not just a vessel; it is a symbol of God's call for everyone in their life. We can stand here at the shore, comforted by the firm ground we have to stand on, and yet, deep within us, we know God is calling us to do something more.

Yet, it is trying, that first step to leave the shore behind and trust fully in God's promises because it happens to feel stable. That is where we can see, where we can prepare, and where we can decide to stand as spectators. But God has something better in store for each one of us than standing on the beach. It is out in the water, where we must learn to trust him, even though we cannot even see what lies before us.

In this journey of faith, there are three kinds of believers: those standing on the shore, those hanging onto the edge of the boat, and those stepping inside, actually stepping, and deciding to jump completely into their trust. The ones who stay on the shore may have already witnessed miracles; they may have seen God's hand working in someone else's life. They may even believe the promise given by God. However, their belief becomes passive and they hesitate to jump maybe due to fear or uncertainty. Then some grab the boat as one foot is in and the other is out, living between commitment and hesitation. They want to follow God, but it's a hard thing for them to let go of that comfort completely, and they land up in a place of indecision, neither wholly committed nor entirely distant. Then there is this third class that has actually gotten into the boat and cast away all doubt, willing to go wherever God should lead them. They know God's calling isn't an invitation, but a command. Getting into the boat meant losing control, believing God would carry them over what was yet to come. This is the faith God seeks, that does not stumble nor retreat but walks boldly in the confidence that He is in charge.

Today, I urge you to step into that faith, to enter the boat completely in reliance on God's plan, even if it requires leaving behind what feels safe.

As Jesus said to his followers, "Let's go across to the other side," he wasn't really referring to taking a boat ride but rather on an inner journey of faith: "Trust in Me. Have faith. Trust Me to take you safely through anything you might face." This crossing is therefore symbolic for transition from knowing about God's power to being initiated into experiencing it firsthand. "Let's go on the other side" is a call to step out of our comfort zones, break free from indecision, and step forward even when we hit the unknown.

The journey, however, was not smooth. A storm hit, and as waves began to beat against the boat, the disciples bore with the kind of fear that crept into their hearts. They cried out, fearful and alarmed, forgetting for a moment that Jesus was there with them. But don't we become just like the disciples at times? As storms and challenges face us, we can let our first impulse and reaction become fear, even panic in the face of experience, yet know that Jesus is by our side. We may wonder if we will live if we have in us whatever the situation demands, or if God has left us to ourselves.

But Jesus was in that boat the whole time. His perspective hadn't changed-their focus had. And so it is with us, as storms rage around us. It's easy to get distracted by the terrific wind, and we forget God's words over the waves.

Fear displaces our peace. But Jesus highlights the storm, reminding us that His power is far greater than any trial we are ever called into. The storm is real, yes, but so is God's presence, power, and promise to bring us safely to the other side. What creates fear and doubt arise not from the overwhelming nature of the storm but from when our attention turns from God's power to our weaknesses.

There, our spiritual eyes have to open. We need to be reminded that God's presence is not just beside us but inside of us. It is the one who navigates the boat, leads us away safely through the storm if we let Him. Faith does not deny that there are challenges around; it is the decision to make a choice to trust God in the midst of those challenges. It is always about knowing that even though the journey may be uncertain, God's promises are sure and unchanging.

When we're in the storm, we have a choice: either let fear control us or let faith sustain us. Jesus' response to the storm was simple yet profoundly deep. He calmed the waves, but before this took place, He had some stern words for His disciples: "Where is your faith?" And He asks us today, as He asked them, "Where is your faith? "The invitation to cross is not a promise of a quiet, uneventful journey; it's a promise that God is with every wave, every storm.

We may have storms, but we are never alone in them. Standing on the shore, or perhaps hanging on to the edge of the boat, Jesus calls us inside, fully.

He invites us to trust not only when the waters are calm but when the waves rise. He invites us to believe, not only in His words but in His presence with us through every high and low. The journey to the other side is a journey of faith; it's there that we learn to depend less on our strength, and more on God's constant love and power.

The question remains, will we stay on the shore, or will we step into the boat knowing God goes with us? Let's choose today to leave the shore behind, to cast off doubt and hesitation, and to move forward in full faith. Let's trust that God's hand is upon the boat, guiding us through every storm and that His promise - to reach the other side - is a promise we can run on. Let us be men and women of faith and not of fear as we press on into the unknown, knowing He will see us through.

Luke 8:22 – "Let's Go to the Other Side of the Lake": Faith and Obedience

In reflecting on the words of Luke 8:22: "Let's go across to the other side of the lake," I realize the depth of Jesus' invitation. This was not a simple instruction; it was a call on someone to step out from their comfort zone by faith and not to step back into the security of what they knew but embrace the uncertainty that awaited him or her. Jesus invites His disciples and through them, us to trust Him totally when the destination isn't clear and when the journey is difficult. This command to "go to the other side" says much about our way of walking in faith, taking us often from our comfort zones into deeper waters.

Consider how they reacted to what he had told them:. They didn't argue with Him or haggle. They didn't ask to have a road map leading to where they were going, that it wasn't going to be bumpy. They just did. Their immediate obedience sets an example for us all. There are times when God gives us the instruction to do something, and we are never informed of the why. He just says to follow Him. This is the essence of discipleship - not just listening but responding to God's call with a willing and open heart. The disciples' response to Jesus' demand provokes questions about our preparedness to respond. Are we as ready to respond, or do we hang on to the shore, waiting for guarantees?

Jesus' words, "the other side," carry a meaning much greater than geography. To the spiritual, "the other side" symbolizes a development, transformation, and unveiling of God's plan in your life. Leaving to the other side may mean leaving out of the comfort zone and familiarity. It could mean giving up old Molds of thinking or divesting oneself from the fear and doubts that have kept him in a state of stagnation. But doing so opens us up to the grand plan that God has prepared. The road may be blurry, but the hope was that on the other side lay the life He wanted for them. It was on the other side that they became like Christ and more responsive to His will for them.

The road that was to take them on to the other side was seldom easy. As they embarked with Jesus, before long the disciples found themselves caught up in a raging storm.

Waves crashed over the boat, and fear was beginning to settle above their faith. In these turbulent moments, it is normal to feel afraid. However, the story goes on to remind us that Jesus was in the boat with them. He hadn't left them to face this storm alone and never leaves us to face our storms alone. Every step of our journey, He is there to guide us, even as the waves rise and the winds howl. This storm that the disciples faced tells us a little bit about the challenges we all face in our own lives—times of trial, moments of uncertainty, and seasons of doubt.

What's so beautiful about this account is the assurance it offers. Jesus being in the boat did not promise a storm would not come, but he promised they would not go alone. This is part of the promise of his presence in our journey. He cannot promise to calm the storm in all areas, but he promises his peace and strength to endure it. He assures us we are safe with him, no matter how threatening the waters may seem around us. Faith isn't the absence of fear; it's the choice to trust that God is greater than whatever storm we're facing. And it's a reminder that no matter how fierce the storm, He has promised to bring us safely to the other side.

I want to leave you with that as I close. Consider this in your own life: What does "the other side" mean? Perhaps it is a new stage of spiritual growth, a step forward in obedience, or a release from fears that have held one back. Whatever it might be, it is Jesus's call to "go to the other side" and choose His promises over our fears, trusting in His presence more than our fear of the storm.

We are reminded here that Jesus promised us not only a smooth journey but that we will safely reach our destination. His word assures us that no matter all these problems, we'll make it if we hang on to our faith in Him. With each trial and every storm, God reminds us of his promises. That journey to the other side is not a journey we make alone; no way, it's a journey with Jesus at our side to lead us, strengthen us, and keep motivating us as we go along. He promised to take us through, and His promises are unbreakable. Let's remember in those overwhelming waves, the destination is certain, not because of our strength but because of His faithfulness.

Let's hear today the words of Jesus. "Let's go to the other side of the lake" is more than a call; it's a promise - a promise that if we follow Him we trust in His guidance, He will take us to where we need to be. The storm may rage, but with Jesus in the boat, we are secure. As we undergo the trials of life, let's take this to heart. Let us remember faith greater than fear, trust greater than doubt, and confidence in His presence above all things. No, nothing can separate us from the love of God that is in Christ Jesus our Lord. And with Jesus at the helm leading the way, that dark unknown other side is not only possible—it's a certainty.

Prophetic Call to Enter the Boat Without Delay

Today, I feel the necessity to share this prophetic word- the word of urgency, the word to call us to action. God, in His invitation, is stern yet urgent; He is calling us to get into the boat and step into His purpose and His plans. So many of us are standing on the shore, watching, waiting, unsure what to do next. But the word today says: Now's the time. God has for us much better things but we will not have them while lingering in a place of indecision or comfort. We remain with our feet still on the shore, perhaps fearing the tug into deeper waters, but we do not know the richer life to which God invites us by coming into His vessel and trusting ourselves to His guiding Half-measures are no longer permitted in the Kingdom of God. The time to act is now before the moment passes and the opportunity fades away.

When I say these words, all I can be reminded of is the grace that has already been overpowered by us. Grace is something we do not need to search and seek; God has given it freely available to us now. That's not an issue of a lack of grace; it's an issue of recognition and response from our side. God has blessed us with all that we need to walk out onto the water, step out of shore, to keep moving forward in faith. I want all of you to see this grace - this open door, this divine invitation to trust in His plan. Now if it's an open door, an open invitation, that means we have got to respond to it. But let each of us embrace this grace, and recognize it to be what it is to live completely in God's plan.

And there is always peril in hesitation. To those who find themselves holding onto the side of the boat, unwilling fully to plunge in, comes a warning here. Indecision keeps us in a weak spot, not quite all the way onshore and not really in the boat. We are on the periphery, neither here nor there. We miss the security and direction of being fully aligned with God. Spiritual stagnation can result from such a position of indecision, feeling disconnected from God's presence, and not knowing one's purpose. It brings us to the scullery of doubt and terror, where our faith is rung weaker rather than being made stronger. The decision to step fully into the boat and COMMITTING FULLY TO GOD'S CALL has attached to it the surety and clarity that only He can achieve. Where we are located - God totally - then our faith grows and we become.

Even within the condition of uncertainty, God is not desolate of us. One of the most reassuring aspects of this prophetic message is God's promise to be with us. He is in the boat guiding us, keeping us safe on the other side. No matter what troubles and trials come our way, He is right there in the midst of the storm and does not leave us. We are safe in His hands, and our walk with Him is not without struggle. For our confidence that He will be with us should make us move forward, to believe that whatever may come, we are safe in His presence. God's promise to be with us is not just a promise for this moment but a commitment. His faithfulness is unwavering, and so it becomes our anchor when things seem crazy and don't make sense. With God around, we can face any storm with confidence knowing He will bring us through.

To the others already in the boat, I say this: let go of doubt. Even as we are in the boat, we fear and doubt God's plan. We cry out in anxiety, wondering if we are safe, wondering if loved. Remember that Jesus is with us. Amid the waves, He did not leave, nor will He leave. Panic and fear will find no room in our lives because the Creator of the universe is in this boat with us. His ways can be considered as less than ours to be tested and said, but our God is greater than our fears. Here, in the very heart of the difference, we must stick to that truth when the journey is arduous. Giving up our doubts, and believing Him, is what distrusting God means. Believe Him when His promises are stronger than the storms.

This is a day of encouragement and reassurance because God's call is urgent and full of love. He doesn't push us forward with reckless abandon; He invites us into His purpose, promising His presence along the way. Step in, dear child; let the vessel hold us fully as we move on. Trust that we are taking a divine step into a plan that has uniquely been designed for each one of us. This is its own set of trials, mercifully filled with His guidance, His grace, and His love that remains unchanged. Let's respond to that great prophecy with faith rather than fear, commitment rather than hesitation, and trust over doubt.
I pray you will find it in your heart to step out onto the water. Get out of the shore. Step fully into the boat and into the journey that God prepared for you. Let God's presence be deep, His guidance powerfully shows itself, and trust that with God in the boat, you will arrive at the other side.

Lessons for a Life of Faith and Trust

As I close these final reflections, my heart beats with a strong prayer that each one of you may more fully drink in and understand it to be an absolute commitment to God's plan. The walk with Him demands a person who can commit wholly and be willing to take trust in His plan, as well as an open heart to what He shall lead us in. God's plan is not a path we walk; it is the ground foundation of our lives. It is already laid out for the serenity and good times but also for the storms and tests. It is only possible to walk with Him when we give ourselves totally to His will, giving up all our ideas and agendas and embracing the divine call He has placed on our lives. Such commitment is not a decision taken overnight, but it is rather a daily choice, a decision to let God lead.

One of the most important faiths in this journey is probably faith over fear. I know that fear is always going to find its way into our lives and creep in at times when we are uncertain or struggling. Fear might be natural, but it must never have the last word in our lives. We are called to overcome fear with faith. We stand firm in the confidence that God is greater than any objection that would come our way. In other words, it does not mean we will not feel fear, but it will not dictate our actions. And faith allows us to have the courage to trust God and believe that He is with us in every trial and guiding us through every storm. He is the One who quiets the roaring winds and calms the raging waters. Let fear rise within us to hold onto God, lean more into His promises, and trust in the unthinkable strength of His might over our anxieties.

Another lesson I'd like you to take with you today is that you live your life in recognition of God's grace already working in your life. So many times we wait for signs, for a moment of assurance before taking that step forward. But God's grace has been given to us in abundance. His provision, His love, and His Spirit are there with every breath we take. Yet rather than waiting upon God for his grace to become victorious within us, we're called to act on it. Imagine the freedom this brings, equipped for what's ahead, prepared for the journey ahead by God. This is not grace we wait to receive; this gift we must live out actively. Let it propel you forward, confident that what you need has already been given by the One who knows you better than you know yourself.

Each one of us needs to be spiritually ready. As the disciples were waiting for Jesus, we too must be watchful, our hearts and spirits open and ready to listen to His call. Being ready is not just listening to the word but acting boldly and with conviction. In a distracted and doubting world, spiritual preparation is a form of discipline that allows one to live a life of constant nourishment of the relationship with God. It's making room in life for Him so that when He calls, we do not have any excuse to make Him wait any longer. When our spirits are tuned to the voice of God, we can even hear Him amidst silence or challenge. Being spiritually prepared means that we don't just hear the Word; we live it, letting it change every aspect of our lives.

But finally, I want to leave here today with all of you to teach on trusting in God's timing. Perhaps this is one of the toughest lessons to learn to trust in God's timing because we live in a world that tells us to speed up and to look for instant results and answers. However, the Lord's timing is in another realm-a holy schedule where He usually tests our patience and faith. The storms will come and go, and the seasons will change, but His moment is always apt. Walking by His schedule brings peace into uncertain situations. God's plan develops at exactly the right moment, neither a second too soon nor a second too late. With such a basis of trust, trusting in His timing means that He can accomplish His purpose for us, at a pace even we may not be able to fully comprehend, yet that will bring us to the deep well of fulfilling, joyful places. The fact is undeniable: He is never in a hurry but is always on time.

In every one of these lessons - commitment to God's plan, faith over fear, noticing the grace, spiritual readiness, and trusting His timing-we see a path for living fully in His presence. May these truths well up in your heart, helping to guide you as you walk with Him. God has called us not to a life of comfort, and ease, but to a life of purpose and connection with God. May we respond with open hearts, ready to follow, knowing He walks with us each step of the way.

7th November 2024 Ghana
Dr Antony Walto,

A prophet of the highest God. He has ministered in our church 'Higher Heights Christian Embassy in Kumasi, Ghana. His ministry is marked by strong Teaching, Prophecy and Notable deliverance.
God's word in his ministry is very defining and graceful. He has also ministered in our international leadership summit.
God has always given him a strong grace for church leaders and has defined many ministers' lives in a remarkable way. He brings freshness in charisma and direction in a very transforming way.
We can confirm the Grace of God on His life as a minister sent for this end time and to the body of Christ. Many churches in Ghana have benefited from his ministry in Ghana.
I recommend him to as many would need his ministry. For His Kingdom.

Dr Ben Christopher Don
Senior Minister.
Higher Heights Christian Embassy & Global coalition of ministers Network. Ghana

Chapter 8

14 April 2018 Kampala. Uganda.

Is your temple a den of robbers? Day 3

Is Your Temple a Den of Robbers?

I stand before you today to reflect on a message that demands introspection and transformation. It is more than a sermon; it is a spiritual wake-up call for each of us to confront the state of our "temples." Jesus' words in Matthew 21:13 ring loud and clear:
"My house will be called a house of prayer, but you are making it a den of robbers."

Today, I invite you to examine the temples of your lives—your hearts, minds, and bodies. Are they sacred spaces of prayer and devotion, or have they become overrun by worldly distractions? Picture the temple in Jesus' time, bustling with merchants and money changers, its holy purpose overshadowed by greed and corruption. Now, think of your own life. Are there "tables" that need to be overturned? Are there "robbers" that need to be cast out? Jesus' cleansing of the temple was not an act of anger but of divine love—a call to restore holiness and reverence. And today, that call is extended to us. He stands at the door of our hearts, ready to enter, but He will not dwell in a space cluttered with sin and distraction. Will you make room for Him?

Sermon Preached by the Prophet

As I delivered this message in Kampala, Uganda, I was struck by the universality of Jesus' challenge. Whether in Uganda, the United States, or any other corner of the world, the human heart faces the same struggles. Materialism, greed, and misplaced priorities creep into our lives and churches, turning sacred spaces into dens of robbers.

I shared personal reflections from my travels—stories of churches where worship has been overshadowed by commerce, and individuals whose spiritual lives have been consumed by worldly pursuits.
I asked the congregation, "When Jesus looks at your temple, what does He see? Is it a house of prayer or a marketplace of distractions?"

The Holy Spirit was present in that gathering, moving hearts and stirring spirits. I reminded them that just as Jesus cleansed the temple, He is ready to cleanse our lives. But the first step must come from us. We must be willing to identify the "tables" that need to be overturned—the habits, distractions, and sins that prevent us from fully experiencing God's presence.

Jesus' actions in the temple were not just about physical cleansing; they were about spiritual restoration. He declared that the temple was meant to be a house of prayer, a place where God's presence could dwell and His glory could be revealed. In the same way, our lives are meant to be temples of the Holy Spirit—sacred spaces where God's love and power can manifest.

Biblical Quote: Matthew 21:13, "My house will be called a house of prayer, but you are making it a den of robbers."

The words of Jesus in Matthew 21:13 are a profound reminder of God's expectations for His people. The temple was meant to be a place of communion with God, but it had been corrupted by greed and distraction.

This verse challenges us to examine our own lives. Have we allowed worldly concerns to take over our spiritual spaces? Have we turned our hearts into dens of robbers? Jesus' actions in the temple show us that cleansing is necessary for restoration. When He overturned the tables, He was making room for prayer, healing, and divine presence.

The transformation of the temple also serves as a symbol of spiritual renewal. Just as Jesus restored the temple's sacredness, He can restore our lives when we surrender to Him. But this requires action. We must actively remove the "robbers" in our lives and dedicate ourselves to prayer and worship. Only then can we experience the fullness of God's blessings.

Prophetic Message

The message I bring to you today is both a challenge and a promise. It is a call to purify your temple, to cast out anything that hinders God's presence. The Holy Spirit is ready to dwell within you, but He cannot share space with sin and distraction.

"Throw out the robbers," I declared to the congregation in Kampala. "Make room for God." This is not just about avoiding materialism or greed; it is about reclaiming your spiritual identity. You are a temple of God, a sacred vessel created to carry His presence. Do not let anything defile that temple.

The promise is this: When you cleanse your temple, miracles will follow. Just as Jesus healed the blind and lame after clearing the temple, He will bring healing and transformation to your life.
But you must take the first step. You must be willing to confront the "tables" in your life and overturn them in faith.

Reflection and Application

The story of Jesus cleansing the temple is not just a historical event; it is a personal call to action. Each of us is a temple of the Holy Spirit, and it is our responsibility to keep that temple holy.

Personal Reflection: Take a moment to examine your life. Are there distractions, habits, or sins that have taken the place of prayer and devotion? What are the "tables" that need to be overturned?

Acting on Faith: Cleansing your temple requires action. Dedicate time to prayer, repentance, and reflection. Identify the areas of your life that need change, and take concrete steps to address them.

Restoring Sacredness: Remember that your body is a temple of the Holy Spirit. Keeping it pure and dedicated to God allows His presence to dwell within and work through you.

Transformation Through Obedience: Just as Jesus restored the temple's sacredness, He can restore your life. But this requires obedience and a willingness to let go of anything that hinders your relationship with Him.

Daily Application: Commit to maintaining your spiritual temple through regular prayer, repentance, and seeking God's guidance. By keeping your temple holy, you create space for God's presence and blessings in your life.

Today, Jesus is calling you to cleanse your temple. He is ready to enter, to bring healing and transformation, but He will not force His way in. The choice is yours. Will you make room for Him? Will you allow your temple to become a house of prayer?

Let us respond to His call with faith and obedience, knowing that when we do, miracles will follow. Just as He restored the temple in Jerusalem, He can restore our lives, filling them with His presence and glory. **Amen.**

PUERTO RICO

GRACE INTERNATIONAL BIBLE UNIVERSITY Maryland, Baltimore, USA
Office of the Founder, Chancellor, and President Bishop Prof. Rudolph Q. Kwanue, Sr., PhD
Founder and President, Rudolph Kwanue University Pipeline, Wein Town Community, Monrovia, Liberia
Letter of Attestation
To: Apostle Dr. Anthony Walto
Date: November 12, 2024
Subject: Testimony for Walto's Walk With Word Worldwide Without Walls

Dear Apostle Dr. Anthony Walto,
On behalf of Grace International Bible University and Rudolph Kwanue University, it is my honour to provide this testimony in recognition of your dedicated service and spiritual impact since joining our institution in 2018. Since your appointment as a board member, your role in providing invaluable advisory support has been marked by unwavering wisdom, profound faith, and exemplary leadership.
Your commitment to spreading the teachings of Yahweh has not only enriched our institution but has also strengthened the spiritual journeys of countless believers. Your guidance has been a blessing to all who have had the privilege of learning from you.
As you prepare to release your book, Walto's Walk With Word Worldwide Without Walls, I am confident that it will serve as a powerful resource for Christians around the world.

Your collection of insights, drawn from ministry experiences across nations, captures a depth of understanding that will guide, inspire, and empower readers in their faith journey.

Thank you, Apostle Dr. Walto, for embodying Yahweh's love and for your steadfast devotion to the ministry.

Your work continues to bless and transform lives, and it is a privilege to stand with you in this calling.

May Yahweh's abundant grace be upon you always.

Blessings,

Bishop Prof. Rudolph Q. Kwanue, Sr., PhD

Founder, Chancellor, Grace International Bible University Founder and President, Rudolph Kwanue University

Www.rkuclr.org

Address: Pipeline, Wein Town Community, Monrovia, Liberia Phone: +231-555-878358

Email: rkuinfo77@gmail.com

Chapter 9 –

26 August 2022
Dubai, United Arab Emirates
Emirates Accommodation

"Jesus went up on a mountainside and called to him those he wanted, and they came to him." Mark 3:13

Responding to God's Call

So let's talk about what it really means to respond to God's call. When Jesus calls his disciples, he's not calling them to be his friends for the moment or the season he's inviting them into a life of purpose, service, and transformation. It must be the most direct divine invitation ever extended to each one of us - not just to be close to Him, but to live for Him, following His ways and bringing his love and truth to a desperate world.

This call is an individual one - a specific calling, and such a strong one. Just like He called His disciples one at a time, calling them by name, God does the same for us. You are not here by chance. God has a purpose for you, and he's calling you to step into it, but His call is not taken lightly; it is a call that meets us right within the heart of examination because it asks us whether we are ready, prepared to let go of our plans and trust in Him?"

This is the start of a life that has faith, sacrifice, and love for God, which will be much bigger than our ambition. When Jesus decided to call His disciples, He did it on a mountainside, away from the noise, at elevation. The mountainside is distant from all the troubles of the world, far from all distractions, and becomes a place where one can connect with God. And there, in that still quiet place, Jesus made His call known. For us, this mountainside can be a place of spiritual clarity, where we step aside from the fray of our daily lives and listen to God's voice. He is calling each of us to your mountainside, a place of peace and perspective, where you can hear with your heart exactly what He intends for you.

Are we willing to give up our comfort and distractions for Him? God called us not only to follow Him but to be transformed by Him. We may have things we'd rather not leave; maybe there are challenges that we are not ready for, but in answering God's call, we will find His presence, His guidance, and His strength. God doesn't call the equipped; He equips the called. He will give us the bravery we need, the wisdom we seek, and the love that will hold us through.

It is a journey, and the stepping-stone begins with faith-a decision to trust Him, even when the way isn't clear, to believe in His purpose, even when the path isn't clear. The loveliest part of this call is that it is a call to ministry and service. God doesn't call us for personal purposes; He calls us to serve others, to spread His love, to share His message, and to be a light in the dark places of life.

You and I are called to be part of something so much greater than who we are today; the divine mission goes beyond the boundaries of our life span and reaches around to the lives of others.

Heeding God's call brings us the privilege to become His hands and feet and to bring hope where there is despair and faith where there is fear. Then, what is asked is not if God is calling us but rather whether we are ready to respond to that call. Are we prepared to take a step out in faith, casting down our fears to trust in God's lead? The call may come in moments of stillness or perhaps by the urgings of the Holy Spirit within our hearts. It may be a quiet whisper or a nagging nudge, but however it comes, it requires a response. God is patient, but He will have an answer.

He called us out of our comfort zones and placed upon our shoulders a life not about ourselves, but Himself; nourished by His word and empowered by His Spirit. Responding to God's call also requires transformation. Let God reorder everything: priorities, dreams, and even relationships. Jesus did not call the disciples just to stay there in their comfort; He called them into a journey that would take them to new places, people they never knew, and situations they never expected.

This is discipleship - being ready to follow Him wherever He would lead us, for His plans are far better than anything we might think up for ourselves. That's a walk of faith - and with faith comes testing.

Still, in that testing, God does not falter nor fail in His call. In other words, He does not go out, call us, and then leave us to our own devices. Instead, He walks with us, strengthens us, and prepares us for every step of the way.

We know those uncertain days when seemingly everything appears to be too much, yet in those moments, God's call becomes our anchor. He brings us back to our reason for starting and whom we are following.

It brings us back to that initial moment of commitment, when we first said "yes" to Him and found that within that nourished courage to move. Let's reflect on how we can respond to God's call while looking at the disciples. They were ordinary people with ordinary lives, but Jesus called them into something out of this world. And they left everything behind to follow him. The call to follow was without sacrifice - it demanded everything from them while giving them a life of purpose, a life that would change the world. Today, that same call is spoken to us. We are not to depart from our homes or our workplaces, but with the same fervour, commitment, and readiness to respond we are called upon to follow Jesus; we should not take it for granted nor deal with it lightly, nor treat it without reverence. His invitation is a gift and a blessing that gives our lives meaning and direction. Every time we respond to the call of God, we enter into His purposes for us, and Mold our lives according to His will, and what He ordains for our futures. There is no greater calling than living for Him as He would have us live - in His ways and a vessel of His love.

This is our purpose, our mission, and our reason for being. And so today, I am asking you to listen closely to His voice. Seek him with all your heart, asking what purpose he has for you, and if he determines the time to inform you, ask him promptly: "Yes" with all that you are. Trust him to equip you, guide you, and walk with you in every step. Accept the call, for in serving Him you are fulfilling the very reason for your existence.

Called for a Purpose: Embracing God's Divine Invitation

Today I am led to share with you the depth and magnitude of the sense of being called by God. When we mention a calling, we start assuming something great, maybe something far away or for another. But I want you to know that each one of us has been chosen for a reason, for a purpose, and that purpose is divinely crafted by God Himself. He calls us, just as He called His twelve disciples to join Him on the side of the mountain. That was no accident; no random selection. His call is intentional, a choice by the One who knows us completely, who understands the gifts he has placed within us, and who sees the potential that perhaps we are not seeing in ourselves.

The call is not to belief but a mission. For God calls for a purpose; there is always a plan involving our faith, obedience, and commitment. Jesus did not simply call the disciples to stand beside him and watch; he called them to work, to spread the word, and to bring hope, healing, and freedom to others.

And so He is exhorting us, too, to do more than just the hearing of the Word; we must respond actively, boldly step out in faith, be able and willing to put our trust in Him, and permit His power to work through us. Each time we respond, we bring ourselves back in line with His will set before us.

Now, when we answer God's call, we are not simply supposed to muddle through it ourselves. Rather, as He empowered his disciples, having authorized them over the demons and the healing of stricken people and having spoken with authority, He empowers each one of us likewise in facing our path. It is not only an invitation but also a conferring authority - a spiritual power that allows us to fulfil the mission He has laid before us. God does not call without equipping, nor does He send you without preparing you. Whatever He asked you to do, big or small, He gave you the strength, wisdom, and courage as well to be able to achieve it. This empowerment, not of our doing but a gift of God, reminds us that when called, we are never alone.

Having received such divine empowerment even we are prepared to face challenges. He, Himself, faced rejection, scepticism, and even doubt. So will it be with us? When the world does not comprehend our calling or question our mission, we just have to remember that even our Savior went through that. He was misunderstood by those closest to him, and mistreated by his own community but pressed on knowing that His calling was greater than the opinions or misunderstandings of others. We will also meet those times when our calling feels heavy or not underlined.

The journey, by no means, is an easy road, but we always walk guided by God's hand. When we doubt, let us remember that our strength does not come from people but through the affirmation of God.

And as we journey, we do not go by ourselves but as one in the same flock. We are all tied together by unity, which is what God called us into. Just as Jesus called twelve to be the cohesive unit that mutually strengthens and supports each other, we are part of an even bigger community. Our call does not happen in isolation but is somehow knit in with the lives and callings of others. We are part of God's family, and his community, and it is in unity that we find strength. A divided house can't stand, and a divided community of believers cannot fulfil its purpose. Our differences are not barriers; they are part of the tapestry God has woven together. Each of us brings a unique gift, and a unique perspective, but it is only in unity that we can completely fulfil God's plan for us and for those to whom we are called to serve.

Unity is important because the work we are called to do is far greater than anything any of us can do alone. It requires us to lay down personal ambitions, pride, and even preferences to come together under a common mission. The mission Jesus entrusted to His disciples, and the mission He entrusts to us today, is to bring the light of God's love into a world that so desperately needs it. This unity is a source of power to build much good in the reflection of God's love, mercy, and grace as we move forward united in purpose.

It's not just a strategy - it's a testimony to the world about what God's family looks like and how his love can bridge any divide and bring together hearts willing to serve.

Just like that, when God calls, we enter a life of purpose, into a different type of life that goes beyond personal goals or worldly ambitions. God's call is sacred and when responded to makes one part of His divine work as vessels to bring healing, hope, and transformation. The authority given to the disciples; the empowerment of casting out darkness and bringing in light, God extends as well to us. But we need to give over our agendas and trust completely in His. There are going to be those moments that are a challenge, but we know that we are "complete in Him," that we are unified and doing something much bigger than anything we could ever do for ourselves.

So today, I invite you to look inward and reflect on God's call for your life. He has called you by name, chosen you, and given you a purpose that only you can fulfil. Step into this calling with the confidence that He has equipped you, that He has empowered you, and that He has placed you within a community of believers walking alongside you. Together, let's walk into this holy plan, help one another in our wanderings, and step forward knowing we're all part of something eternal, part of something that would be to the glory of God, and something sacred.

Answering the Call: The Divine Selection on the Mountainside

Upon reflection of Mark 3:13, it tells me that the picture is bright; it says Jesus is standing on the mountainside and calling to himself those he wanted. Not a call of chance but rather a choice. It was an invitation by Jesus to join him in this journey that would change life. And those called didn't just walk behind; it was called for something much more profound and divine. And just as He called them, so I believe that He calls each one of us with purpose and intent. There is a personal nature in His call- a personal nature that reassures us that we are not overlooked, but are seen, known, and wanted by God Himself. We invite people into life anything but an ordinary life of closeness with our Creator, a life of mission and purpose.

I picture Jesus taking up his place on the mountain, a place set apart where all else fades and there is only God. Mountains, according to scripture, are usually representational of moments of revelation and transformation, places where the encounter with God reaches deep. Moses was sent up a mountain to receive the commands; Elijah found God's still, small voice in the silence of a mountain. And here, Jesus takes this setting to draw His disciples into a holy place, away from the crowd, away from the mundane. In this mountainside, we have a metaphor for each of us, urging us to live above the throngs of the world and invite something deeper within ourselves to God.

It is on this "mountainside" that we become clear and aware of what life is all about and recognize God's clearer voices above any other noise.

The moment Jesus called His disciples, they never had the question of hesitation; they responded immediately. This obedience to the call is crucial. A reminder that when God speaks, we respond that matters. Those Jesus called left what they were doing and came to Him. Their obedience was the first act of faith. It revealed their readiness to take on the unknown - to trust this One who is calling them more than they were acquainted with their lives. And this obedience wasn't merely a step in time, but rather the start of a lifestyle. We are called to consider how we respond when God calls us in our lives. Are we quick to respond or slow to answer, under the influence of fear or doubt? Jesus is not looking for half-hearted followers. He looks for totally committed followers who leave their comfort zones and entrust to His will for them what they could hardly imagine.

Calling, then, is not solely obedience; it is an invitation into intimacy. Jesus wanted not merely the disciples to follow Him but to be with Him, to walk alongside Him, learn from Him, to share in His life and ministry. It is the same for us. God's call is not an assignment into a role nor the completion of some task but is rather an invitation to a relationship, a journey beginning with being close to Him. True discipleship is closeness with God, knowing His heart, voice, and presence. When we answer His call, we don't just embark on a mission. We move into a relationship.

All our acts spring from this closeness, being the first of His, before service and ministry. It is in His presence that we are transformed, renewed, and readied for the work ahead.

But, however much intimacy there will be, there will also be empowerment. God doesn't call us without equipping us. Jesus empowered His disciples when He called them. They were empowered to cast out demons, heal the sick, and proclaim the Kingdom of God. Authority and power went well beyond human possibilities with them. This empowerment was necessary for them, and it is necessary for us. God's call comes with divine resources, with a power that's not our own. We do not look at our strength or wisdom; we are filled with His Spirit, guided by His hand, and empowered with everything we need to accomplish what He set before us. This is His promise to us: that He will never leave us alone, that He will be with us every step of the way, and will empower us to fulfil the purpose He has given us.

As we obey His call, we step into a purpose greater than ourselves, a mission that reverberates through all eternity. They had no inkling of the impact they would have on people's lives, inspiring across generations and into the time to come. Nor do we. We may feel small and inadequate, even maybe unprepared, but answering God's call puts us in a timeless story, written before the times started. Our willingness to respond, to say "yes" to His call, becomes part of that story. That will make it a testimony of His faithfulness, reflect of His love, and a witness of His power.

So encourage me: As I encourage myself, listen for His voice. Let us go up to that "mountainside" where, without din, we shall hear Him, and where we shall find no noise to attend to but the call of our Savior, with which we must respond. Let us respond with obedience, an open heart to intimacy, and faith which believe He would empower. God is calling every one of us not because we have a spotless record, not because we have all the answers, but because He has chosen us and sees in us the potential to be His hands and feet in this world. This is where He bridges the comparison between who He is and the difficulty of challenges, doubts, and fears. His call brings along with it a promise: He will be with us, He will equip us, and He will use us for His glory.

As we respond to His call, may we not be changed merely by the mission but by our relationship with the One who called. Let us walk in His steps. We can do this, empowered by His Spirit and committed to His purpose, knowing we are part of something way, way bigger than ourselves. Chosen, called, and empowered are the words in those texts. And in that truth, we find the strength to step forward, to walk in our purpose, to bring His love, His grace, and His truth into a world that desperately needs it.

Prophetic Message: Embracing God's Unique Call and Empowerment

Today, I feel an intense desire to share with you a message that comes straight from my heart—a word from the prophets to the heart of each one of you—to stop and think, to seriously look at the life you are living. I want you to consider whether you really heard God's call for you. And if you do hear God's call, I want to challenge you honestly to assess whether you are living according to that call. It's not a matter of hearing the distant whisper and nodding in passing. God's call is an invitation into a life of purpose, a life uniquely crafted for you alone. But it involves not just recognition but action—an uncompromising commitment to walk in His ways, living out the purposes designed specifically for you.

God's call is customized, unique, and fitted according to the person whom He has created you to be. When Jesus chose his twelve disciples, he did not collect them at random. The ground for choosing each disciple was handpicked for a reason-for their gifts, strengths, and weaknesses-all woven into God's divine plan. And so is the case with each one of us; he singles us out, and His calling is as deliberate as well. His call is not to just exist but to live, to be of significance, to make an imprint upon the world, to touch lives. He calls you by your name; He knows the gifts which have been placed within you and experiences you've been through, coming together in the beautiful and complex design of His purpose for you.

And with that calling comes a season of preparation, and it's precisely in this place that most of us feel the weight of God's work in our lives. At times, the path of fulfilling purpose does not always seem clear; it sometimes makes one feel as if they are taking detours or roadblocks. But hold your horses and let me assure you; every single one of those steps is part of God's preparation. Just as Jesus had given his authority to the disciples when he had taught and formed them, so too are we being melded by every experience, every hardship, every moment of learning and growth. God is preparing us for greater works than which we can presently think. This period of preparation is of great importance. It Molds our character and strengthens our faith so that upon His full commission, we become capable of doing His work with integrity, strength, and divine authority.

On this journey, you may be disappointed to discover that not everyone understands or supports your mission. Like Jesus, we might face rejection, doubt, or even scorn from people around us. God just does not get a life driven by faith and purpose - a life that is set apart by God. But remember, the world's opinion is but of the moment, whereas God's approval is forever. Jesus Himself was doubted and resisted, but he stood firm because His cause was from the Father, and that's all that mattered. In like manner, we fix our eyes not on what is seen, but on what is unseen, because what is seen is transitory, but what is unseen is eternal. The worldly rejections shake us not nor dilute our passion, because we focus on what is set before us: His purpose. We serve before an audience of One, and the approval of One is all we need.

As we embark on this leap into our call, we are not alone when we go out. God, with His big wisdom and love, gave us the final source of guidance, power, and comfort, which is the Holy Spirit. We are not talking about just some feeling and acknowledging it in theory; He is our living source of power, constant companion, and divine empowerment, equipping us to face every obstacle, every moment of doubt that we may encounter on the road. When we feel weak or unprepared, remember that the Holy Spirit is in us, empowering us for the job ahead. He fills our weaknesses with His strength, so our doubts become courage and our hesitations take on bold steps of faith. We are not sent into the mission field without the power to accomplish it; we are backed by the full authority of Heaven itself.

Thus, let this prophetic word be a word of encouragement as well as wake-up call. Reflect on your calling, just take some time to assess how you are doing. God called not only to observe but to engage; not only to follow at a distance but to walk hand in hand with Him for a life of purpose. Chosen, prepared and empowered in our God. It wouldn't always be easy and there would be trials to remind and challenge your faith. His promise, though, stays strong. He has chosen you; He has equipped you; He will be with you every step along the way.

Take heart and step boldly into this calling. Embrace the preparation, accept the challenges, and lean into the Holy Spirit's guidance. In such a moment as this, you can be aligned totally with God's purpose, trusting that with His Spirit within you, there's no mountain too high, no valley too deep, and no storm too fierce that would stop you from fulfilling what He has called you to do. God has much more for you than that which seems to oppose you, and the approval of His means all to you.

Live your life in the confidence that He called you, stand firm in doubt, and walk each day empowered by the Holy Spirit because He knows you walk in the purpose set by the Creator Himself.

Lessons on Spiritual Unity

Reflecting on the vital lessons of unity within the body of Christ, I am now compelled to share how deep and essential it is for each of us to understand and embrace the call to unity in our spiritual lives. Therefore, this is where the church itself has come to rest-together with one another building our foundation in our local settings and in the wider body of Christ- the very heart of our faith community. Unity is not beautiful just on its own. No, it rests as bedrock where God's Kingdom can move ahead incrementally, powerfully, and graciously. We are a force for good, healing, and transformation when united. But division, when it takes hold, can so weaken the blow of the church and break the rhythm of God's work that flows among us.

What words of Jesus are those that state, "A house divided against itself cannot stand." Such was the fact stated there, not just concerning individual families, but also concerning the family of the believers.

Division is an insidious threat that, left unchecked, can nibble away at the core of the church from within. It's easy enough to observe how disunity affects us-it divides our hearts, distracts us from our purpose, and ultimately diminishes our collective strength. A divided church loses its influence and power; it becomes unable to stand as the bright light God intended it to be in a world that desperately needs His hope. We cannot afford to let disunity sap our strength or dim our purpose.

Unity, however, is the way of spiritual growth and improvement. It's here where we stand strong, courageous, and strengthened as one. We are all exposed to these adversities and temptations in life individually, but together we make up a spiritual family that uplifts, upholds, and strengthens one another. Unity in the body of Christ, therefore means looking beyond individual preferences or small differences. This calls us then to a far greater thing: a common purpose, a common love, and a common mission in Christ. As we come together in his name, putting aside all personal agendas and focusing on what God wants, we create an unbreakable stronghold of faith. It is then that we can do great things both within our communities as well as outside of them.

But unity doesn't come by itself. For this reason, reconciliation often requires intentionality, and sometimes it is needed with reconciliation. We are called to reconcile differences; we are called to seek peace where there is discord and to heal wounds that may cause separation. Such is a call to reconciliation, not only unto ourselves but all the body of Christ.

In our families, in our congregations, and in our relationships with fellow believers, we are encouraged to be agents of peace, to forgive as we have been forgiven and to seek understanding above all. Taking that first step across the lines of misunderstanding or hurt—be it base misconceptions or past pains—gives room for God's healing to operate and His love to grow. Reconciliation strengthens us as community, binds us closer, and makes us more efficient in our mission.

Under this message is a great truth: we are actually working for one mission-one purpose-that is the spreading of the gospel and bringing others to the love and salvation of Jesus Christ. This would bind us together as believers and straighten us with the heart of God. When we are focused on this mission, seeing ourselves part of a far greater thing than our individual roles, then unity becomes possible. We will come to realize that our differences are not barriers but rather unique contributions to the larger vision that God has for His people. Every member of the body has a place, purpose, and value in God's Kingdom. By embracing this truth we learn to appreciate one another and are spurred on to work together, as we strive to bring other people into the saving grace of Christ.

This is unity in the body of Christ and it is not uniformity. The meaning is not that we must all think, act, or worship alike. But a spirit of harmony demands of us a commitment to strive together despite this diversity. God creates us each unique, each with our own special gifts, talents, and perspectives, and it is in that diversity alone that lies the true beauty of this church. Coming together, bringing with them a part of ourselves, we create that fuller, richer, and more dynamic expression of God's love. Our unity is made strong not by erasing differences, but by celebrating them so that each part contributes toward the whole in a manner that brings glory to God.

As we live out that unity, then we are doing exactly what Jesus prayed for us in John 17:21, where He said, "that all of them may be one, Father, just as you are in me and I am in you." This reminds each of us that our unity is a reflection of God's unity and is a very powerful testimony to the world of His love. Then we have seen in the way we stand together, the way we love each other, and the way we strive for a common goal-some manifestation of God's Kingdom bursting into earth. We are one society marked not by conflict nor by opposites but by love, compassion, and purpose.

Let us, then, commit ourselves to life together, constructing a spiritual family strong, sturdy, and focused on the mission to which God has entrusted us. Instead, let us forgive, reconcile, and understand one another. Let's work together, build up, and lift each other so that we may become examples of God's love and grace to those around us. From now on, we shall remember that strength lies in unity and this becomes the vital part of the mission entrusted upon us. Let us be that united, steadfast, and loving community of people living out God's will to bring others into His family. As a community, together we can do more than we ever could alone.

REV DR ANTONY WALTO 19/11/2024

To God be the Glory great thing He has done. I and Back to God family Church international are excited hearing of the publication of your new book.

Dr Antony Walto is such a wonderful minister of the Gospel. His passion for the kingdom work is outstanding. These few years of knowing him, he has been a blessing to me and the church. His love, patience is great. We pray you reach out to millions. This book will surely turn lives around. Congratulations

Viennatech Innovations GmbH.
Laura Müller
Tynk.com to 2024-06-07 07:39:29 UTC
Jeremiah Bansah

Rev. Dr. Antony Walto

Grace & Peace, may all blessings be unto you as you read these words. It is a great honour to be chosen by God our Father & Creator and to be used by Him in the earth. When we allow ourselves to embrace our "difference" from just being a "born again "Christian" believer," and we step into the calling wherewith we have been called, our lives take on a new meaning. We are called to be above & beyond the "normal" phase of just living life day to day. When God calls us to be an extension of Him here on earth, we take on His Character, His Nature, His Power & His Glory! Many are called, but few are chosen. Whom God has called, He has predestined & ordained us to carry out His will here in the earth. It is knowing that He wants us to present to others His Love, His Power & perform signs, wonders & miracles following (Mark 16:20) When we allow ourselves to be conformed to His Likeness, yield to His Unction and see the world the way He sees it, He will do the work with us and confirm His Word.

As a "Prophetic" people, we are to live a life that is filled with signs, wonders & miracles just as Jesus did when He walked the earth physically. Our lives are to reflect the miraculous the same as breathing air. It should be a "normal" for us as God's Chosen. Many are called, but few are chosen. That's what the Word of God tells us. We must identify what that means and learn how to execute that to the fullest & satisfaction of our God.

The earth is travailing & groaning waiting for the "Manifestation of the Sons of God!" When we look around our world today, the earthquakes in divers places, the wars, rumours of wars, the hatred & death.....that is like labour pangs for a woman in the "birthing process." The pangs come & go until that which she is carrying is birthed. Looking Spiritually, God wants to "birth" a thing in the earth, but He needs our help to do it. We are not the ones doing the work, He is. That leads to something that is to be taken to another level in the things of the Kingdom of Heaven.

We must not only see Him as "only God," when we do that, we allow ourselves to only pray to a God that seems distant, we must embrace the fact that He has called us "Sons of God!" The enemy of our souls only recognizes the "Son of God!" Not the Prophet, not the Apostle, not the Pastor, the Teacher or the Evangelist! He knows that only the Son has the same Authority in the earth as the Father. Jesus Himself said "If you have seen me, you have seen the Father because He & I are One!"

Jesus walked the earth as "Son of Man," although we know He is the Son of God, man was His earthly form, but His Authority makes Him Son of God. Let us now embrace what & who we are in Him, in the Kingdom of heaven & who we are in the earth and be the "Extension & Re-presentation" of God our Father in the earth. Let us exude His Character & Love. When we love others, we want to see them, healed, made whole, delivered & empowered to live a happy, healthy prosperous life.

Let us be one with the Father as Jesus is One and we will be that 3 Fold Chord that is not easily broken! Father bless you greater!

Prophetess Cleautrice Smith
cleautrices@gmail.com, Los Angeles, CA

Chapter 10 –

"Sermon of Public Meeting: Day 1, Kenya" - 25 May 2014

"For where two or three gather in my name, there am I with them." - Matthew 18:20

Introduction

I stand before you today with a profound sense of awe and gratitude, reflecting on the promise Jesus made in Matthew 18:20: "For where two or three gather in my name, there am I with them." These words are more than a scripture; they are a divine guarantee of His presence among us whenever we come together in faith and unity. As I recall the powerful gathering in Kenya on 25 May 2014, I am reminded of the transformative power of this promise—a power that changes lives, heals hearts, and brings heaven closer to earth.

That day in Kenya was a testament to the sanctity and strength of fellowship. The gathering wasn't in an elaborate sanctuary but under the open sky, with believers from different walks of life united by one purpose: to seek the Lord together. As I stood before them, I could feel the anticipation in the air, a tangible hunger for God's presence. And as we lifted our voices in worship, the truth of Matthew 18:20 came alive. His presence wasn't a distant hope—it was a reality we could feel, hear, and see.

The promise of Matthew 18:20 isn't just about numbers; it's about the intention of the heart. Jesus didn't set a high threshold for His presence. He didn't demand thousands or grand ceremonies. Instead, He said, "Two or three." This is the beauty of His promise—it's accessible to all of us, no matter where we are or how many gather. What matters is that we come together in His name, unified by faith and a shared desire to glorify Him.

That day in Kenya, I spoke about the power of gathering. I told the people that unity in Christ is like a river that flows stronger as more streams join it. Each of us is like a stream, and when we come together in His name, we create a mighty current that carries blessings, healing, and miracles. I urged them to see their fellowship as more than a routine gathering but as a divine appointment where heaven meets earth.

As we worshipped, I saw barriers breaking down. I saw people who had been weighed down by burdens begin to lift their hands in surrender. Tears flowed freely as hearts were opened, and the Spirit moved among us. It was a reminder that when Jesus is present, transformation is inevitable. The broken are mended, the weary are strengthened, and the lost are found.

Jesus' words in Matthew 18:20 also serve as a call to action. Gathering in His name isn't just about physical proximity; it's about spiritual unity. It's about setting aside differences, offenses, and distractions to focus solely on Him.

That day in Kenya, I saw a glimpse of what the body of Christ is meant to be—a community bound by love, faith, and a shared mission to glorify God. The unity of the believers created an atmosphere where miracles could happen, and indeed, they did.

I remember a woman in the crowd who had been battling an illness for years. She came forward during the time of prayer, and as we laid hands on her and prayed in faith, her countenance changed. She testified later that she felt a warmth, a healing touch, that she knew was from the Lord. This wasn't the work of man; it was the manifestation of Jesus' promise. He was with us, moving among us, touching lives in ways only He can.

The promise of Matthew 18:20 also challenges us to live with expectancy. When we gather in His name, we should come with the expectation that He will show up, that He will move, that He will speak. Too often, we approach gatherings with routine or scepticism, forgetting that we are meeting with the King of Kings. That day in Kenya, the believers came with expectancy, and they were not disappointed. The Spirit moved because their hearts were open, their faith was alive, and their focus was on Him.

As I reflect on that gathering, I am reminded that the power of fellowship extends beyond the event itself. The impact of that day rippled out into the community. People who had never spoken to each other before left as friends. Families were restored, and the testimonies of God's goodness continued to inspire others long after the meeting ended.

This is the power of gathering in His name—it not only transforms the moment but creates a lasting legacy of faith and unity.

But this promise also comes with a responsibility. When we gather in His name, we are not just receivers of His presence; we are carriers of it. We are called to take what we experience in fellowship and bring it into our daily lives, our families, our workplaces, and our communities. That day in Kenya, I reminded the believers that the church is not confined to four walls. It is wherever two or three gather in His name—at home, in the marketplace, on the streets. Wherever we go, we carry His presence with us, and we are called to share it with the world.

As you reflect on Matthew 18:20, I challenge you to examine your approach to fellowship. Are you gathering with expectancy, ready to experience His presence? Are you united with those you gather with, or are there barriers of offense or division that need to be addressed? Remember, His promise is activated when we come together in His name, in unity and faith.

Let this promise also encourage you in your personal walk with Christ. Even when you feel alone, remember that His presence is not limited to physical gatherings. When you call on His name, He is there. Whether you are with others or in the solitude of your prayer closet, His Spirit is with you, guiding, comforting, and empowering you.

Today, as I look back on that day in Kenya, I am filled with gratitude for the reminder that Jesus is always faithful to His promises. His presence is not a distant hope but a present reality, available to all who seek Him. And as I stand before you now, I invite you to step into this promise. Gather in His name, not out of obligation but out of a deep desire to encounter Him. Come with expectancy, with faith, and with unity of purpose. And as you do, watch how He moves in your midst, transforming lives, healing hearts, and drawing us closer to Him.

"For where two or three gather in my name, there am I with them." These words are a gift, a guarantee, and a guide. May we hold onto them, live by them, and allow them to shape our gatherings, our relationships, and our faith. Let us be a people who gather not just to be in each other's presence but to be in His presence, united by His love, and empowered by His Spirit.

Sermon Preached

As I stood before the congregation that day in Kenya, I felt the weight of the message I was about to deliver. It was not just a sermon; it was a divine reminder of the power inherent in unity, faith, and the promise of Jesus' presence. I began by sharing stories from my own ministry—moments where small gatherings of believers became the epicentre of extraordinary breakthroughs. These were not tales of grandeur but of faith, of people coming together with a single purpose: to call upon the name of the Lord.

I spoke of times when just a handful of believers gathered in living rooms, under trees, or in small community halls, and yet, heaven responded. These were not moments defined by numbers but by the sincerity of hearts united in faith. "For where two or three gather in my name," Jesus promised, "there am I with them." I reminded the congregation that this promise is as alive today as it was when Jesus first spoke it.

As I looked into the faces of the people gathered that day, I saw anticipation, hunger, and hope. I told them, "It does not matter how many of you are gathered here today. What matters is the purpose for which you are here and the name in which you gather." The congregation nodded, affirming their readiness to receive this timeless truth. I could see their hearts opening as they grasped the significance of Jesus' words in Matthew 18:20.

I emphasized that Jesus' presence is not reserved for grand assemblies or massive events. His promise is for the small groups, the family prayers, the two friends who come together to intercede for a loved one. His presence is not contingent on numbers but on the sincerity of faith and unity of purpose. "Do not underestimate what happens when you gather in His name," I told them. "He is here with us now, moving among us, touching hearts, and listening to every prayer."

To bring this truth to life, I turned to one of my favourite biblical examples: the story of the four friends in Mark 2:1-12. These men, united in their faith, carried their paralyzed friend to Jesus.

They faced obstacles—a crowd too large to navigate and a house too full to enter. Yet, their unity and determination pushed them to climb the roof, break through it, and lower their friend before Jesus. I asked the congregation to picture the scene: the dust falling, the crowd murmuring, and the paralyzed man being gently lowered before the Savior.

"This is what it means to gather in His name," I explained. "It is not always easy. It may require effort, sacrifice, and creativity, but when we come together in faith, miracles happen." I urged them to think about their own lives and their own communities. "Who are you carrying to Jesus? And who is carrying you?" I asked. "Faith is not meant to be a solitary journey. Just as the four friends worked together to bring their companion to Jesus, so must we support one another in our walk with God."

I then turned the focus back to the congregation, challenging them to be a community that uplifts, supports, and strengthens one another. "You are not here by accident," I said. "God has placed you in this church, in this community, to be a light to each other and to the world. When you gather in His name, you become a beacon of His presence. Your unity has power. Your prayers have strength. Do not underestimate what you can do together."

I shared a personal story of a time when I was struggling in ministry, feeling the weight of responsibility and the sting of rejection. It was a small group of faithful friends who gathered with me, prayed for me, and reminded me of God's promises. Their prayers lifted me, their faith strengthened me, and their unity became a channel for God's presence to move in my life. "This is the kind of community God calls us to be," I told them. "A community that stands together in faith, that carries each other to Jesus, and that never gives up."

As the sermon drew to a close, I issued a powerful appeal: "When you gather in His name, come with expectancy. Do not come out of routine or obligation but out of a deep desire to encounter Him. Your prayers have power, your faith has strength, and your unity invites His presence. Approach Him with humility and expectation, and He will move among you."

I looked out at the congregation and saw tears in many eyes. The Holy Spirit was moving, touching hearts, and stirring faith. I asked them to take a moment of silent reflection, to think about the times they had felt alone or discouraged. "In those moments," I said, "remember His promise. You are never truly alone. When you call on His name, He is there. And when you gather with others in faith, His presence is magnified."

Finally, I reminded them that with this promise comes a responsibility. "When you gather in His name, you are not just receivers of His presence; you are carriers of it. You are called to take what you experience here and bring it into your daily lives, your families, your workplaces, and your communities. Be the hands and feet of Jesus to those around you. Let your unity in faith inspire others to believe."

I ended with a prayer, asking God to strengthen the bonds of unity among them, to fill their hearts with faith, and to make His presence known in every gathering. As the prayer concluded, the congregation erupted in worship, their voices rising in unison, a powerful testament to the promise of Matthew 18:20.

That day in Kenya was not just another meeting; it was a divine encounter. The words I spoke were not mine but His, given to remind His people of the power of unity and the assurance of His presence. As I stepped down from the pulpit, I felt a deep sense of peace, knowing that His promise had been made real to those who had gathered.
And now, I say to you, wherever you are reading this, remember His words: "For where two or three gather in my name, there am I with them." Let this promise guide your gatherings, strengthen your faith, and inspire you to seek His presence. Whether you are in a grand cathedral or a humble home, know that when you gather in His name, He is there, ready to move, ready to heal, and ready to bless.

Biblical Quote: Matthew 18:20, "For where two or three gather in my name, there am I with them."

As I reflect on the profound truth of Matthew 18:20, my heart swells with gratitude for the unshakable promise it carries. Jesus' words, "For where two or three gather in my name, there am I with them," are not merely a statement; they are a divine assurance. They remind us that our faith journey is never meant to be solitary. In these words, Jesus calls us to the sacred act of gathering, to bring together our hearts, our prayers, and our burdens in His name. And when we do, He promises to meet us there.

This verse is not about numbers; it is about purpose. It is not about the grandeur of the assembly but the unity of hearts aligned in faith. It assures us that whether we are in a vast congregation or a small prayer group, the presence of Jesus is the same. He meets us with His transformative power, ready to heal, restore, and guide. This promise is a cornerstone of Christian fellowship, a beacon of hope that encourages us to come together in His name.

I have often spoken about how faith is meant to be shared. It is a journey where we lean on one another, carry each other's burdens, and uplift one another in prayer. Jesus' words in Matthew 18:20 remind us of this sacred truth. When we gather, we create an atmosphere where His presence becomes tangible, where the power of collective faith can move mountains.

I recall moments in my ministry when just two or three believers gathered in prayer, and the presence of the Holy Spirit was undeniable. These gatherings were not large, but they were powerful. In their simplicity and sincerity, they became spaces where miracles unfolded, hearts were mended, and lives were transformed. It is a testimony to the fact that Jesus does not look at the size of the crowd; He looks at the unity of their hearts and their devotion to His name.

The beauty of this verse lies in its emphasis on unity. When believers come together, their collective faith becomes a force that invites God's power to manifest. It is in these moments of unity that we see the extraordinary happen. I have witnessed it countless times: healing that defies medical explanation, peace that surpasses understanding, and breakthroughs that only God could orchestrate. These moments are a reminder that when we gather in His name, we create an environment where miracles are possible.

Unity is not always easy. It requires humility, forgiveness, and a willingness to put aside personal differences for the greater purpose of worship and prayer. But when we achieve it, the rewards are immeasurable. The presence of Jesus in our gatherings brings healing to fractured relationships, restoration to weary souls, and hope to those in despair. It is a powerful reminder that God works through the unity and devotion of His people.

Every gathering centred around God is sacred. Whether it is a Sunday service, a Bible study, or a small group of friends praying together, these moments carry divine significance. Jesus' promise to be with us when we gather in His name elevates these meetings from routine events to holy encounters. It challenges us to approach every gathering with reverence, expectation, and a heart open to His presence.

I often remind congregations that fellowship is not just about being physically present; it is about being spiritually engaged. It is about coming together with a shared purpose, to worship, to pray, and to seek His will. When we do this, our gatherings become a reflection of heaven on earth, a place where God's glory is revealed and His love is felt.

In today's world, it is easy to become isolated. The demands of life, the distractions of technology, and the busyness of our schedules often pull us away from meaningful fellowship. Yet, Matthew 18:20 challenges us to prioritize gathering with other believers. It reminds us that there is power in community, in coming together to support one another and to seek God's presence.

I have seen how prioritizing fellowship can change lives. It creates a support system, a network of believers who encourage one another, pray for one another, and walk alongside one another in faith. It strengthens our spiritual journey and reminds us that we are not alone. Jesus is with us, and so are our brothers and sisters in Christ.

There is something extraordinary about the way God works through unity. When we gather in His name, we are not just individuals seeking Him; we are a collective body inviting His presence into our midst. This unity creates a fertile ground for His power to be revealed. It is in these moments that we see His ability to heal the sick, to restore broken relationships, and to bring hope to the hopeless.

I remember a gathering where just a handful of us came together in prayer. The atmosphere was charged with faith, and as we lifted our voices in unison, the presence of the Holy Spirit became palpable. Prayers were answered, chains were broken, and lives were changed. It was a testament to the promise of Matthew 18:20, a reminder that when we gather in His name, He is truly with us.

As I reflect on this verse, I am reminded of the responsibility it places on us as believers. It is not enough to know that Jesus is present when we gather; we must act on that knowledge. We must approach every gathering with expectancy, ready to experience His presence and to be vessels of His love and power.

This is not just a call to attend church services or prayer meetings; it is a call to live in constant fellowship with other believers. It is an invitation to create spaces where Jesus can move, whether in our homes, our workplaces, or our communities. It is a challenge to be intentional about gathering in His name, knowing that when we do, His presence will transform our lives.

Matthew 18:20 is more than a verse; it is a way of life. It invites us to embrace the power of community, to prioritize fellowship, and to trust in the promise of His presence. It reminds us that faith is not a solitary journey but a shared one, where we come together to support one another, to pray for one another, and to experience the fullness of God's love.

As we gather in His name, let us do so with hearts full of faith, with a spirit of unity, and with an expectation of His presence. Let us be reminded that wherever two or three are gathered, Jesus is there, ready to heal, to restore, and to transform. And let us carry this promise with us, creating spaces where His presence can be felt and His power can be revealed.

May this verse inspire us to gather often, to pray fervently, and to live in the assurance that Jesus is with us, always.

Prophetic Message

As I stood before the congregation that day, I felt the undeniable presence of the Holy Spirit guiding me. The message that stirred in my heart was one of assurance, hope, and divine power—a call to each believer to embrace the promise of Jesus' presence. With Matthew 18:20 as our anchor, the words flowed from me not as my own, but as a divine prompting: "You are not alone in this gathering. Jesus is here, moving among us, ready to transform hearts and lives."

From the first moment, I urged those gathered to lift their eyes beyond the physical, beyond the crowd around them, and to sense the tangible presence of Jesus. "Where two or three are gathered in His name, He is there among them," I reminded them. This is not a distant hope or a conditional promise; it is a certainty that when we unite in His name, we invite Him to dwell among us. I asked them to feel it—not with their emotions alone, but with their spirit—to recognize that the King of Kings had entered into their midst.

“His presence changes everything,” I declared with conviction. "When Jesus is in the room, sickness must flee, despair turns to hope, and chains of bondage are broken. His presence is not a passive one; it is active, alive, and transformative.” I reminded them that it wasn’t about the size of the gathering but the sincerity of their hearts. Even a few faithful hearts, united in His name, can create an atmosphere ripe for miracles.

The Spirit spoke through me as I emphasized the power of unity. "When believers stand together in faith, they become an unshakable force, capable of overcoming any obstacle." I could see the congregation begin to understand that their strength did not lie in their individual abilities, but in their collective faith. The walls of Jericho fell not because of a single voice but because of a unified shout of faith. The early church grew and thrived because the believers were of one heart and mind. Unity is not just a principle; it is a spiritual weapon, a divine strategy for breaking through every barrier.

“Each one of you here today,” I continued, “is a part of this great tapestry of faith. When you weave your prayers, your worship, and your faith together, you create something indestructible. It is this unity that invites Jesus to walk among us. It is this unity that amplifies His power.”

“Approach Him with humility,” I urged. "When you come before God, come not with pride or presumption but with open hearts ready to receive. The blessings of God are not for the boastful or the self-reliant; they are for those who acknowledge their need for Him.”

I asked the congregation to reflect on their hearts as they stood before the Lord. “Are you ready to receive? Are you prepared to lay down your burdens, your doubts, and your fears at His feet?” The Spirit moved as I spoke, and I could see many begin to release their worries, their tears flowing freely as they surrendered their cares to God.
With expectation comes preparation, I reminded them. “Do not come before God half-heartedly. Come with anticipation, with faith that He will meet you, heal you, and restore you. When you expect Him to move, your heart is ready to recognize and receive His blessings.”

“Jesus’ presence does not leave us the same,” I proclaimed. “When He is among us, He transforms us. He brings clarity to our confusion, strength to our weakness, and grace to our struggles.” I spoke of how His presence illuminates the darkest corners of our hearts, revealing hidden wounds and offering healing.

"Whatever you walked into this place carrying—whether it be guilt, shame, fear, or pain—He stands ready to lift it off your shoulders. All He asks is that you bring it to Him."

I shared testimonies of those who had experienced this transformation, recounting how their lives were forever changed after they encountered the presence of Jesus in gatherings just like this one. These stories were not meant to elevate me as the preacher but to magnify the power and faithfulness of God. "If He did it for them," I declared, "He will do it for you. He is the same yesterday, today, and forever."

As the prophetic message reached its crescendo, I assured the congregation of God's faithfulness. "God's blessings will follow those who gather in His name with sincere hearts. Miracles await those who believe." These were not empty words but a divine promise rooted in Scripture and affirmed by the Holy Spirit. I reminded them that miracles are not always dramatic or immediate but that God's hand is at work in both the extraordinary and the everyday.

"Do not measure His blessings by human standards," I cautioned. "A miracle might be the restoration of a broken relationship, the quieting of a troubled mind, or the strength to face another day. Whatever form it takes, know that it is a sign of His love and His presence in your life."

Finally, I challenged the congregation not to let the promise of Matthew 18:20 remain confined to that gathering. "Take this promise with you," I urged. "Wherever you go, wherever you gather—in your homes, your workplaces, your communities—know that He is there with you. Carry His presence into the world, letting it shine through your words, your actions, and your love for others."

As the Spirit moved powerfully among us, I felt compelled to pray over the congregation, sealing the message in their hearts. "Lord, let these words take root in every soul here today. Let them carry Your presence boldly, trusting in Your promises and walking in unity. May their gatherings be filled with Your power, and may their lives be a testament to Your love."

The prophetic message that day was not just a call to faith but a reminder of the extraordinary promise we have in Jesus. His presence is with us whenever we gather in His name, and through that presence, we are strengthened, transformed, and equipped to carry His love into the world. It is a promise that continues to resonate, calling each of us to live in unity, faith, and expectation of His miraculous power.

Reflection and Application

As I reflect on the promise of Matthew 18:20—"For where two or three gather in my name, there am I with them"—I feel a deep stirring in my spirit to call each of you to examine your gatherings, your prayers, and your fellowships. Are they centred around Jesus, or have worldly distractions crept in unnoticed? This is not a question meant to accuse but to awaken. It is a gentle reminder to return to the heart of what it means to gather in His name: to focus on Him, to invite His presence, and to allow His Spirit to guide and transform.

When we come together in faith, it is more than a meeting—it is a divine encounter. But how often do we treat our gatherings as routine, letting our hearts wander to worldly concerns or personal distractions? I have seen it in my own journey: moments when the sacredness of fellowship was diluted by the noise of life. Yet, each time I refocused my heart on Jesus, the transformation was undeniable.

I urge you to reflect on the gatherings in your life. Are they saturated with prayer, worship, and the expectation of His presence? Or have they become a social event, devoid of the spiritual depth that invites Jesus to move among you? Remember, His promise is not tied to the size of the gathering but to the unity of purpose and the sincerity of faith. Even a small group of believers, united in His name, has the power to shake the heavens and bring His kingdom to earth.

When we gather, it is not enough to simply show up. Our faith requires action—participation in prayer, worship, and service. Each time we kneel in prayer or raise our voices in worship, we are actively inviting Jesus to take His place among us. I have witnessed firsthand how active participation transforms not only individuals but entire communities. It is in these moments that barriers are broken, hearts are healed, and lives are renewed.

In Kenya, during a gathering of faithful believers, I saw this truth come to life. People arrived with burdens so heavy that their physical posture reflected their spiritual weight. Yet, as they lifted their voices in unity, the atmosphere changed. Tears flowed, hands were raised, and the tangible presence of Jesus filled the room. By the end of that gathering, those same people walked out with joy, hope, and a renewed sense of purpose. Their active participation had opened the door for Jesus to work among them.

I challenge you to examine your role in your spiritual gatherings. Are you a spectator, or are you actively contributing to the collective faith that invites His presence? Let your prayers be fervent, your worship be wholehearted, and your heart be expectant. In doing so, you become a vessel through which His Spirit can flow, blessing not only you but those around you.

Unity is not merely a concept; it is a divine mandate. Jesus prayed for His followers to be one, just as He and the Father are one.

This unity is not about uniformity but about aligning our hearts with His purpose and supporting one another in faith. When we come together in love and unity, we reflect the very nature of God to the world.

I have seen the beauty of this unity in action. In one gathering, a group of believers banded together to support a family in need. Their collective faith and love brought not only material provision but also spiritual encouragement. That family, once on the brink of despair, found hope in the tangible expression of God's love through His people. This is the power of unity—a force that transcends individual efforts and magnifies the impact of God's mission.

I encourage you to foster this unity in your own communities. Reach out to those who are struggling, pray with and for one another, and let your gatherings be a place where God's love is made manifest. Remember, where two or three gather in His name, He is there, and His presence will amplify your efforts.

Jesus' promise in Matthew 18:20 calls for a posture of humility and devotion. When we gather in His name, we are standing on holy ground. It is not a time for personal agendas or superficial interactions but a sacred moment to seek His face and align our hearts with His will.

I have learned through my own walk with God that humility opens the door for His presence. When we approach Him with a contrite heart, acknowledging our dependence on Him, He meets us with grace, strength, and guidance. I have seen gatherings transformed when people let go of their pride and come before Him in humility. The barriers that once separated them—pride, judgment, and self-interest—melt away in the light of His presence.

As you gather, let your hearts be focused on Him. Prepare yourself through prayer, clear your mind of distractions, and come with a spirit of expectancy. Trust that He will meet you where you are and that His presence will bring renewal and growth.

The principles of Matthew 18:20 are not confined to formal gatherings; they are meant to permeate every aspect of our lives. Here are practical steps to live out this promise:

- **Regular Participation in Prayer Meetings**: Commit to being an active part of your church or faith community. Your presence matters, and your faith contributes to the collective strength of the gathering.

- **Building Relationships Within the Faith Community**: Invest time in fostering meaningful connections with fellow believers. Share your struggles, celebrate your victories, and walk together in faith.

- **Seeking God's Presence in Every Aspect of Life**: Whether in your home, workplace, or personal time, invite Jesus to be present. Make prayer and worship a daily habit, creating a space for His Spirit to dwell.

- **Living with Expectancy**: Approach each day with the belief that God is at work in your life. Look for His hand in the ordinary and trust Him for the extraordinary.

- **Reflecting God's Love**: Let your actions be a testament to His presence in your life. Serve others selflessly, forgive freely, and show kindness to all.

As I look back on the gatherings where I have witnessed the promise of Matthew 18:20 come to life, I am reminded of the profound truth that Jesus' presence changes everything. It is not about the numbers but the hearts united in His name. It is about the faith, love, and humility we bring to the gathering that invites His Spirit to move. Today, I call on you to reflect on your own gatherings. Are they centred around Jesus? Are they marked by unity, humility, and active participation? If not, let this be the moment to recommit, to refocus, and to realign your heart with His promise.

When you gather in His name, know that He is there with you—ready to heal, restore, and transform. Let this truth shape your prayers, your worship, and your interactions with others. And as you go forth, carry His presence into the world, creating ripples of His love and power wherever you go. For where two or three gather in His name, He is there among them, and in His presence, all things are possible.

Conclusion: Walking in the Fulness of God's Call

Now that I have reached the end of this book, my heart is full of thanks and hope as I realize that the journey we have walked together through these pages is just the beginning. Having written this book has been a commitment to share what God put inside me-been repeated so much that He amplifies it through years of ministry, travel, and countless encounters in His spirit's power. Each teaching, each story, each prophetic word I've spoken was to open your heart and prepare you for the path God has lain before you.

I have come to know one thing beyond a shadow of a doubt: God's calling is real. It's not an abstract concept; it's a tangible invitation from the Creator of the universe to you personally. Not only is it for you to experience His presence but to walk hand in hand with Him, empowered by His Spirit to achieve the purpose He has specifically crafted for your life. This calling isn't for a few; it's for every person who wants to live fully for Him. As you reflect upon what you have read, I urge you let those words settle into your spirit. Let His truths become your own, and let His Spirit guide you in the steps He's asking you to take.

Through all the teaching and journeys I've walked through together with you, may you have sensed a pull within you to draw closer to the intimacy with God. It is there-- this nearness to God's heart-- where all else starts.

The closer we get to Him, the more like Him we become- by His nature shaping us, by His love healing us, by His power making the coward within us bulge out into boldness. From this intimacy in relationship, we start walking under His authority and influence those around us while doing the work He has placed in our hands.

My heart's cry is that every believer grows up into Christ, because we do not merely believe in Christ; He has fully loved us, fully empowered us, and fully sent us, making us actually the body of Christ on earth, to be His hands and His feet. And there's just that kind of surrender and that kind of love that must happen as a result of the work of the Holy Spirit in us. In every place I have gone and every life I have touched, I have seen the incredible transformation that occurs when people experience God personally and yield to His leading. He lives in you, right here, right now, to lead you into the fullness of your call. When you close this book and walk out of the room, never forget that you are not walking alone. God is with you and promised to lead you step by step in every step. Anchored, continue searching for Him with all your heart and hold onto the trust that His promises to you are sure. No matter the roadblocks, no matter the fears that try to find their way into your mind, continue to believe God will carry you through every thing and bring you into the purpose He has set before you.

Let this book be a launch, a base on which you can construct a life deeply rooted in God's love, guided by His Spirit, and marked by His power. Walk by faith, knowing God is at work in you, preparing the way before you for great things done in His name. Fill, then, my dear fellow, with the Holy Spirit, and set on fire with passion to steadfastly keep your purpose, for such a journey is rich in promise ahead.

May you continue walking in His light, so sensitive to the voice of His heart, and allow the journey He has prepared for you to be your pilgrimage. It is no greater joy than to know we are loved, called, and empowered by the very Creator Himself. Take His hand, follow His lead, and live out the destiny He has designed for you. It is in Him that you will find everything that you need. It is through Him that the kingdom of God will happen and continue to change your life and those around you forevermore.